ISAIAH

Chapters 1—35

J. Vernon McGee

THOMAS NELSON PUBLISHERS
Nashville

Published in Nashville, Tennessee, by Thomas Nelson, Inc., and distributed in Canada by Lawson Falle, Ltd., Cambridge, Ontario.

Scripture quotations are from the KING JAMES VERSION of the Bible.

Library of Congress Cataloging-in-Publication Data

McGee, J. Vernon (John Vernon), 1904–1988
   [Thru the Bible with J. Vernon McGee]
   Thru the Bible commentary series / J. Vernon McGee.
     p.   cm.
   Reprint. Originally published: Thru the Bible with J. Vernon
McGee. 1975.
   Includes bibliographical references.
   ISBN 0-8407-3273-2
   1. Bible—Commentaries. I. Title.
BS491.2.M37 1991
220.7'7—dc20   90–41340
                                CIP

Printed in the United States of America

1 2 3 4 5 6 7 — 96 95 94 93 92 91

CONTENTS

ISAIAH—CHAPTERS 1—35

PREFACE

The radio broadcasts of the Thru the Bible Radio five-year program were transcribed, edited, and published first in single-volume paperbacks to accommodate the radio audience.

There has been a minimal amount of further editing for this publication. Therefore, these messages are not the word-for-word recording of the taped messages which went out over the air. The changes were necessary to accommodate a reading audience rather than a listening audience.

These are popular messages, prepared originally for a radio audience. They should not be considered a commentary on the entire Bible in any sense of that term. These messages are devoid of any attempt to present a theological or technical commentary on the Bible. Behind these messages is a great deal of research and study in order to interpret the Bible from a popular rather than from a scholarly (and too-often boring) viewpoint.

We have definitely and deliberately attempted "to put the cookies on the bottom shelf so that the kiddies could get them."

The fact that these messages have been translated into many languages for radio broadcasting and have been received with enthusiasm reveals the need for a simple teaching of the whole Bible for the masses of the world.

I am indebted to many people and to many sources for bringing this volume into existence. I should express my especial thanks to my secretary, Gertrude Cutler, who supervised the editorial work; to Dr. Elliott R. Cole, my associate, who handled all the detailed work with the publishers; and finally, to my wife Ruth for tenaciously encouraging me from the beginning to put my notes and messages into printed form.

Solomon wrote, ". . . of making many books there is no end; and much study is a weariness of the flesh" (Eccl. 12:12). On a sea of books that flood the marketplace, we launch this series of THRU THE BIBLE with the hope that it might draw many to the one Book, *The Bible.*

J. VERNON MCGEE

The Book of

ISAIAH

INTRODUCTION

Beginning with Isaiah and continuing through the Old Testament, there is a section of Scripture which is called the prophetic portion of the Bible. That does not mean that prophecy begins with Isaiah, because there are prophecies as far back as the Pentateuch, which was written by Moses. Although the predictive element bulks large in this section, the prophets were more than foretellers. They were men raised up by God in a decadent day when neither priest nor king was a worthy channel through which the expressions of God might flow.

These books of prophecy also contain history, poetry, and law, but their primary message is prophecy. Each writer, from Isaiah to Malachi, is a prophet of God. Today we make an artificial division of the prophets by designating them as the *major prophets* and the *minor prophets*. All of the prophets are in the major league as far as I am concerned—I don't think you can put any of them back in the minors. This artificial division was determined by the length of the book, not by content. Some of the minor prophets are like atom bombs—they may be small, but their content is potent indeed.

These prophets not only spoke of events in the distant future, but they also spoke of local events in the immediate future. They had to speak in this manner in order to qualify for the prophetic office under God according to the Mosaic code. Codes for the priest, the king, and the prophet are given in the Book of Deuteronomy. Note the code for the prophet: "But the prophet, which shall presume to speak a word in my name, which I have not commanded him to speak, or that shall speak in the name of other gods, even that prophet shall die. And if thou say in thine heart, How shall we know the word which the LORD hath not spoken? When a prophet speaketh in the name of the LORD, if the thing follow not, nor come to pass, that is the thing which the LORD hath not spoken, but the prophet hath spoken it presumptuously: thou shalt not be afraid of him" (Deut. 18:20–22). If the local event did not transpire *exactly* as the prophet predicted, he was labeled a false prophet and was so treated. You may be sure that the message of the false prophet is not in the library of inspired Scripture. The prophetic books are filled with events that are local and fulfilled.

If you had lived in Isaiah's day, how would you have known that he was a true prophet? You would have judged him on his local prophecies. He not only spoke of events far in the future, like the first and second comings of Christ, but he also spoke of local things that would happen in the near future. If his local predictions had not come to pass exactly the way they were given, he would have been recognized as a false prophet and stoned.

The prophetic books are filled with local prophecies already fulfilled. All of the prophets gave local prophecies to prove that they were genuine. Remember that a sharp distinction needs to be drawn between fulfilled and unfulfilled prophecy. When any prophecy was first given, it was of course unfulfilled. Since the time the prophecies were given, a great many of them have been fulfilled. One of the greatest evidences that these men were speaking the words of God is that hundreds of their prophecies have been fulfilled—fulfilled literally.

Man cannot guess the future. Even the weatherman has difficulty in prognosticating the weather for twenty-four hours in advance, although he has the advantage of all sorts of scientific and mechanical devices to assist him. The fact of the matter is that no weatherman that you and I listen to so intently would survive as a prophet in Israel!

The law of compound probability forbids man from consistently foretelling the future. Each uncertain element which he adds decreases his chance of accuracy 50 percent. The example of hundreds of prophecies which have had literal fulfillment has a genuine appeal to the honest mind and sincere seeker after the truth. Fulfilled prophecy is one of the infallible proofs of plenary verbal inspiration of Scripture.

Let me illustrate: Suppose I make a prophecy that it is going to rain tomorrow. I would have a fifty-fifty chance of being right. It is either going to rain or it is not going to rain—that is for sure. Now I add another element to my prophecy by predicting that it will begin raining at eleven o'clock in the morning. That reduces my chance of being right another 50 percent, but I still have a 25 percent chance of being correct. But I don't stop there. I not only say that it will start raining at eleven o'clock, but I also say that it will stop raining at three o'clock. I have reduced my chances again and have only a 12½ percent chance of being right. If I keep adding uncertain elements until I have three hundred prophecies, you know they would never be literally fulfilled. No man can guess like that. Only the Holy Spirit of God could give such information. A man would not have a ghost of a chance of being right that many times, and yet God's Word has over three hundred prophecies concerning the first coming of Christ, which have been literally fulfilled.

Why did God give so many prophecies concerning the first coming of Christ to earth? There is a logical and obvious answer. The coming of the Lord Jesus Christ to earth was an important event. God did not want the children of Israel to miss Him. God marked Him out so clearly that Israel had no excuse for not recognizing Him when He was here on this earth.

Let me use a homey illustration: Suppose I am invited to your hometown. You ask me, "When you arrive at the airport, how will I know you?" I would write back and say, "I am arriving at the airport at a certain time on a certain flight. I will be wearing a pair of green-checked trousers and a blue-striped coat. I will have on a big yellow polka dot necktie and a pink shirt with a large purple flower on it. I will be wearing one brown shoe and one black shoe and white socks. On my head you will see a derby hat, and I will be holding a parrot in a cage in one hand, and with the other hand I will be leading a jaguar on a chain." When you arrive at the airport, do you think you would be able to pick me out of the crowd?

When Jesus came to earth more than nineteen hundred years ago, those who had the Old Testament and knew what it said should have been waiting at the inn in Bethlehem or waiting for the news of His birth, because they had all the information they needed. When the wise men appeared, looking for the Lord Jesus, the Israelites at least should have been interested enough to hitch a ride on the back of the camels to take a look themselves. Oh, how tremendously important His coming was, and how clearly God had predicted it!

The prophets were extremely nationalistic. They rebuked sin in high places as well as low places. They warned the nation. They pleaded with a proud people to humble themselves and return to God. Fire and tears were mingled in their message, which was not one of doom and gloom alone, for they saw the Day of the Lord and the glory to follow. All of them looked through the darkness to the dawn of a new day. In the night of sin they saw the light of a coming Savior and Sovereign; they saw the millennial kingdom coming in all its fullness. Their message must be interpreted before an appreciation of the kingdom in the New Testament can be attained; the correct perspective of the kingdom must be gained through the eyes of the Old Testament prophets.

The prophets were not supermen. They were men of passions as we are, but having spoken for God, their message is still the infallible and inspired Word of God. This is substantiated by writers of the New Testament. Peter tells us: "Of which salvation the prophets have inquired and searched diligently, who prophesied of the grace that should come unto you: Searching what, or what manner of time the Spirit of Christ which was in them did signify, when it testified beforehand the sufferings of Christ, and the glory that should follow" (1 Pet. 1:10–11).

Moreover I will endeavour that ye may be able after my decease to have these things always in remembrance. For we have not followed cunningly devised fables, when we made known unto you the power and coming of our Lord Jesus Christ, but were eyewitnesses of his majesty. For he received from God the Father honour and glory, when there came such a voice to him from the excellent glory. This is my beloved Son, in whom I am well pleased. And this voice which came from heaven we heard, when we were with him in the holy mount. We have also a more sure word of prophecy; whereunto ye do well that ye take heed, as unto a light that shineth in a dark place, until the day dawn, and the day star arise in your hearts: Knowing this first, that no prophecy of the scripture is of any private interpretation. For the prophecy came not in old time by the will of man: but holy men of God spake as they were moved by the Holy Ghost (2 Pet. 1:15–21).

It was William Cowper who said, "Sweet is the harp of prophecy; too sweet not to be wronged by a mere mortal touch."

Most of the prophets moved in an orbit of obscurity and anonymity. They did not project their personalities into the prophecy they proclaimed. Jeremiah and Hosea are the exceptions to this, which we will see when we study their books. Isaiah gives us very little history concerning himself. There are a few scant references to his life and ministry. In Isaiah 1:1 he gives the times in which his life was cast: during the reigns of Uzziah, Jothan, Ahaz, and Hezekiah, all kings of Judah. In Isaiah 6 he records his personal call and commission.

The days in which Isaiah prophesied were not the darkest days in Judah internally. Uzziah and Hezekiah were enlightened rulers who sought to serve God, but the days were extremely dark because of the menace of the formidable kingdom of Assyria in the north. The northern king of Israel had already been carried away into captivity.

Isaiah 36—39 records the historical section of the ministry of Isaiah during the crisis when the Assyrian host encompassed Jerusalem. Beyond these few personal sections, Isaiah stands in the shadow as he points to Another who is coming, the One who is the Light of the world.

There are those who believe that Isaiah belonged to the royal family of David. This is supposition and certainly cannot be proven. Likewise it has been stated that he is referred to in Hebrews 11:37 as the one "sawn asunder."

Whether or not this is true, the liberal critic has sawn him asunder as the writer of the book. They have fabricated the ghastly theory that there are several Isaiahs. According to this theory the book was produced by ghost writers whom they have labeled "Deutero-Isaiah" and "Trito-Isaiah." The book will not yield to being torn apart in this manner, for the New Testament quotes from all sections of the book and gives credit to one Isaiah. The critics have cut up Isaiah like a railroad restaurant pie, but history presents only one Isaiah, not two or three.

A friend of mine, who has made quite a study of the Dead Sea Scrolls, tells me that Isaiah is the scroll the scholars work with the most. There is a great section of Isaiah intact, and only one Isaiah is presented. It is quite interesting that the Lord let a little shepherd boy reach down into a clay pot, in Qumran by the Dead Sea, and pick out a scroll that confounds the critics. The Lord will take care of the critics.

Let me illustrate how ridiculous the double or triple Isaiah hypothesis really is. Suppose a thousand years from today some archaeologists are digging in different parts of the world. One group digs in Kansas, another in Washington, D.C., and another group digs in Europe. They come up with the conclusion that there must have been three Dwight Eisenhowers. There was a General Eisenhower, the military leader of the victorious Allied forces of World War II in the European theater. There was another Eisenhower who was elected president of the United States in 1952 and 1956. There was still another Eisenhower, an invalid and victim of a heart attack and of a serious operation for ileitis. This illustration may seem ridiculous to some people, but that is exactly how I feel when I hear the critics talk about three Isaiahs. Of course there was only one man by the name of Dwight Eisenhower who fulfilled all the requirements without any absurdity. The same is true of Isaiah.

The prophecy of Isaiah is strikingly similar to the organization of the entire Bible. This similarity can be seen in the following comparison:

BIBLE	ISAIAH
66 Books	66 Chapters
39 Books—Old Testament	39 Chapters—Law, Government of God
27 Books—New Testament	27 Chapters—Grace, Salvation of God

There are sixty-six direct quotations from Isaiah in the New Testament. (Some have found eighty-five quotations and allusions to Isaiah in the New Testament.) Twenty of the twenty-seven books of the New Testament have direct quotations. Isaiah is woven into the New Testament as a brightly colored thread is woven into a beautiful pattern. Isaiah is discernible and conspicuous in the New Testament. Isaiah is chiseled into the rock of the New Testament with the power tool of the Holy Spirit. Isaiah is often used to enforce and enlarge upon the New Testament passages that speak of Christ.

The historic interlude (chs. 36—39) leaves the high plateau of prophecy and drops down to the record of history. Even the form of language is different. It is couched in the form of prose rather than poetry.

The third and last major division (chs. 40—66) returns to the poetic form but is in contrast to the first major section. In the first we had judgment and the righteous government of God; in the last we have the grace of God, the suffering, and the glory to follow. Here all is grace and glory. The opening "Comfort ye" sets the mood and tempo.

It is this section that has caused the liberal critics to postulate the Deutero-Isaiah hypothesis. A change of subject matter does not necessitate a change of authorship. It is interesting that for nineteen hundred years there was not a word about a second Isaiah. John refers to this section as authored by Isaiah (see John 1:23). Our Lord likewise referred to this section as written by Isaiah (see Luke 4:17–21). Philip used a chapter from this section to win an Ethiopian to Christ (see Acts 8). There are numerous other references which confirm the authorship of Isaiah.

Isaiah prophesied many local events. When Jerusalem was surrounded by the Assyrian army, Isaiah made a very daring prophecy: "Therefore thus saith the LORD concerning the king of Assyria, He shall not come into this city, nor shoot an arrow there, nor come before it with shields, nor cast a bank against it" (Isa. 37:33). Also see Isaiah's prophecy concerning the sickness of Hezekiah in Isaiah 38.

There are other prophecies which were not fulfilled in his lifetime, but today they stand fulfilled. See, for instance, his prophecies concerning the city of Babylon: "And Babylon, the glory of kingdoms, the beauty of the Chaldees' excellency, shall be as when God overthrew Sodom and Gomorrah. It shall never be inhabited, neither shall it be dwelt in from generation to generation: neither shall the Arabian pitch tent there; neither shall the shepherds make their fold there. But wild beasts of the desert shall lie there; and their houses shall be full of doleful creatures; and owls shall dwell there, and satyrs shall dance there. And the wild beasts of the islands shall cry in their desolate houses, and dragons in their pleasant palaces: and her time is near to come, and her days shall not be prolonged" (Isa. 13:19–22).

Further fulfillments relative to Babylon are recorded in Isaiah 47. Excavations at Babylon have revealed the accuracy of these prophecies. More than fifty miles of the walls of Babylon have been excavated. The culture of this great civilization is still impressive but lies in dust and debris today according to the written word of Isaiah. This is one of many examples that could be given. Others will come before us in this study as we proceed through the book.

The New Testament presents the Lord Jesus Christ as its theme, and by the same token Isaiah presents the Lord Jesus Christ as his theme. Isaiah has been called the fifth evangelist, and the Book of Isaiah has been called the fifth gospel. Christ's virgin birth, His character, His life, His death, His resurrection, and His second coming are all presented in Isaiah clearly and definitively.

OUTLINE

I. **Judgment (Poetry), Chapters 1—35**
Revelation of the sovereign on the throne
  A. Solemn Call to the Universe to Come into the Court Room to Hear God's Charge against the Nation Israel, Chapter 1
  B. Preview of the Future of Judah and Israel, Chapter 2
  C. Present View of Judah and Jerusalem, Chapter 3
  D. Another Preview of the Future, Chapter 4
  E. Parable of the Vineyard and Woes Predicated for Israel, Chapter 5
  F. Isaiah's Personal Call and Commission as Prophet, Chapter 6
  G. Prediction of Local and Far Events, Chapters 7—10
     (Hope of future in coming child)
  H. Millennial Kingdom, Chapters 11—12
  I. Burdens of Surrounding Nations (Largely Fulfilled), Chapters 13—23
     1. Burden of Babylon, Chapters 13—14
     2. Burden of Moab, Chapters 15—16
     3. Burden of Damascus, Chapter 17
     4. Burden of the Land beyond the Rivers of Ethiopia, Chapter 18
     5. Burden of Egypt, Chapters 19—20
     6. Burden of Babylon, Edom, Arabia, Chapter 21
     7. Burden of the Valley of Vision, Chapter 22
     8. Burden of Tyre, Chapter 23

  J. Kingdom, Process, and Program by Which the Throne is Established on Earth, Chapters 24—34
  K. Kingdom, Mundane Blessings of the Millennium, Chapter 35

II. **Historic Interlude (Prose), Chapters 36—39**
(This section is probably a prophetic picture of how God will deliver His people in the Great Tribulation, see 2 Kings 18—19; 2 Chron. 29—30.)

A. King Hezekiah and the Invasion of Sennacherib, King of Assyria, Chapter 36
B. King Hezekiah's Prayer and the Destruction of the Assyrian Hosts, Chapter 37
C. King Hezekiah's Sickness, Prayer, and Healing, Chapter 38
D. King Hezekiah Plays the Fool, Chapter 39

III. **Salvation (Poetry), Chapters 40—66**
Revelation of the Savior in the Place of Suffering (There is a threefold division marked by the concluding thought in each division, "There is no peace to the wicked.")
A. Comfort of Jehovah Which Comes through the Servant, Chapters 40—48
(Polemic against idolatry—Help and hope come only through the Servant)
B. Salvation of Jehovah Which Comes through the Suffering Servant, Chapters 49—57
   1. Redeemer of the Whole World, Who Is God's Servant, Chapters 49—52:12
   2. Redemption Wrought by the Suffering Servant, Who Is God's Sheep (Lamb), Chapter 52:13-53
   3. Results of the Redemption Wrought by the Redeemer, Who Is God's Only Savior, Chapters 54—57

C. Glory of Jehovah Which Comes through the Suffering Servant, Chapters 58—66
   1. Sin Hinders the Manifestation of the Glory of God, Chapters 58—59
   2. Redeemer Is Coming to Zion, Chapters 60—66
   (Nothing can hinder God's progress—He will judge sin)

CHAPTER 1

THEME: God's charge against the nation Israel

Chapter 1 is God's solemn call to the universe to come into the courtroom to hear God's charge against the nation Israel.

Isaiah lived in a time of tension. In many respects it was a time of crisis in the history of the world. World-shaking events were transpiring. Catastrophic and cataclysmic judgments were taking place. There was upheaval in the social order.

A new nation had arisen in the north; it was moving toward world domination. Assyria, the most brutal nation ever to put an army on the battlefield, was marching to world conquest. Already the northern kingdom of Israel had been taken into Assyrian captivity. The southern kingdom of Judah was in a precarious position, and an Assyrian army, 185,000 strong, was just outside the walls of Jerusalem.

In this dire, desperate, and difficult day Hezekiah entered the temple and turned to God in prayer. God sent His prophet with an encouraging word. He asserted that Assyria would never take Judah, the army of Assyria would never set foot in the streets of Jerusalem, and they would never cross the threshold of any gate of the city of the great King. But God was preparing another nation, Babylon, the head of gold down by the banks of the River Euphrates; this nation would eventually take Judah into captivity unless she turned to God.

God was giving Judah another chance. In order to establish the justice of His cause, God called her into court; He held her before His bar of justice. He gave her opportunity to answer the charge, to hear His verdict, and to throw herself on the mercy of His court. God invites us into the court to see if He is just. It is well for this day and generation to go into the courtroom and see God on the throne of judgment in this sensational scene.

In the thinking of the world, God has been removed from the throne of judgment. He has been divested of His authority, robbed of

His regal prerogative, shorn of His locks as the moral ruler of His universe; He has been towed to the edge of the world and pushed over as excess baggage. This is a blasphemous picture of God! He is still the moral ruler of His universe. He is still upon the throne of justice; He has not abdicated. He punishes sin.

Isaiah records the principles upon which God judges the nations. God raises up nations, and He puts them down. The kingdoms of this world today are Satan's, but God overrules them. God has permitted great nations to rise, and He has permitted Satan to use them; but when it is time in God's program for certain nations to move off the stage, He moves them off—Satan notwithstanding. Even God's own people, the Jews, are a testimony of the fact that He rules in the affairs of the nations of this world.

There is an expression that keeps recurring in my thinking from the Song of Moses which the children of Israel sang as they crossed the Red Sea. The expression is, "Jehovah is a man of war." Yes, He is! And He will not compromise with sin. He will not accept the white flag of surrender. He is moving forward in undeviating, unhesitating, and uncompromising fury against it. There would be hope today for man if he could say with Isaiah, "I saw also the Lord sitting upon a throne" (Isa. 6:1).

The vision of Isaiah the son of Amoz, which he saw concerning Judah and Jerusalem in the days of Uzziah, Jotham, Ahaz, and Hezekiah, kings of Judah [Isa. 1:1].

First of all, note that this is a vision "concerning Judah and Jerusalem." I am sure that we will not make the mistake of locating either one anywhere in the Western Hemisphere. There is, however, a marvelous application for America today—one that we need to hear and heed.

"In the days of Uzziah, Jotham, Ahaz, and Hezekiah." Uzziah, the tenth king of Judah, became a leper because he intruded into the holy place, which even a king was not permitted to do. However, Uzziah is classed as a good king. Jotham, his son who followed him, was also a good king. But Ahaz, the grandson of Uzziah, was a bad king. Finally,

Hezekiah, the last king mentioned, was a good king. He was the king who asked that his life be prolonged, and God granted his desire. Asking this was probably a mistake on Hezekiah's part, because many things took place during his last years that actually were the undoing of the kingdom.

> **Hear, O heavens, and give ear, O earth: for the LORD hath spoken, I have nourished and brought up children, and they have rebelled against me [Isa. 1:2].**

God begins this prophecy in a majestic manner. This is God's general judgment against Judah. He is calling the world, if you please, to come into the courtroom and listen to the proceedings as He tries His people. God does not do anything in a corner or in the dark. This language is strangely similar to the way Deuteronomy 32 begins: "Give ear, O ye heavens, and I will speak; and hear, O earth, the words of my mouth." When God put the nation Israel in the land, having taken them out of the land of Egypt, He put down the conditions on which He was "homesteading" them in the Promised Land. He called the created intelligences of heaven and earth to witness these conditions.

Now, after five hundred years, God says, "I have nourished and brought up children, and they have rebelled against me." He is ready to take them out of the land and send them into Babylonian captivity. He calls the created intelligences of heaven and earth to witness that He is just and right in His dealings. His charge against them is rebellion. The condition upon which they were allowed to dwell into the land was obedience. They were disobedient; and, according to the Mosaic Law, when a man had a rebellious son, that son was to be stoned to death. God's charge against them is a serious one. As His children, they had rebelled against the Mosaic Law in this connection. In the Book of Deuteronomy note the law concerning an incorrigible son: "If a man have a stubborn and rebellious son, which will not obey the voice of his father, or the voice of his mother, and that, when they have chastened him, will not hearken unto them: Then shall his father and his mother lay hold on him, and bring him out unto the elders of his city, and unto the gate of his place; And they shall say unto the elders of his city, This our son is stubborn and rebellious, he will not obey our voice; he is a glutton, and a drunkard. And all the men of his city shall stone him with stones, that he die: so shalt thou put evil away from among you; and all Israel shall hear, and fear" (Deut. 21:18–21).

This was what the Law did with a prodigal son. The crowd that heard Christ tell of the Prodigal Son was dumbfounded when He said that the father told the servant to kill the fatted calf instead of killing the son! When the Prodigal Son got home, he asked his father for forgiveness, and even before he finished his confession, his father had thrown his arms around the boy, kissed him, and forgiven him. Instead of stripes, the son was given a wonderful feast. God is not only just, but also merciful; but the rebellion of a son is a serious thing. Scripture has a great deal to say about it.

In order to emphasize His charge and break the tension of the courtroom, God indulges in a bit of humor. I trust that you recognize humor in the Bible—it will make you enjoy it a great deal more. I think that when we get into eternity, and get past the time of sin on earth and are finished with the program God is working out at this present time, we are going to have a good time. I think we are going to have many laughs and enjoy many hilarious situations. It does not hurt Christians to have the right kind of humor. God has put a lot of humor in the Bible. A lady, who was a member of a church I pastored, was upset every time I found humor in the Bible. She would make a trip down the aisle and tell me that I was being irreverent. She has been home with the Lord for a long time, and I do hope she has had a couple of good laughs, because she certainly never had them down here. The fact of the matter is, she acted like she had been weaned on a dill pickle. Unfortunately, she never found humor in this life, and she didn't seem to enjoy the Christian life as God has intended us to enjoy it.

The ox knoweth his owner, and the ass his master's crib: but Israel doth not know, my people doth not consider [Isa. 1:3].

This verse is a splendid piece of satire. The two animals that are used for illustrations do not have a reputation for being very intelligent. Neither the ox nor the long-eared donkey has a very high I.Q. The expression "dumb as an ox" is still often used. The donkey does not wear a Phi Beta Kappa key. I should qualify that statement: I admit that I have met a few who do! However, even these animals have intelligence enough to know who feeds them.

When I was a pastor in Texas, there was a grassy vacant lot across the street from the church to which a very poor man with many patches on his overalls would bring his little donkey. While the donkey was grazing, many of the little boys and girls in the neighborhood would ride him, and even the preacher rode him once in a while. When I would get on his back, he wouldn't pay any attention to me—or to anyone else. Late in the afternoon the donkey's owner would come for him. When he came tottering along, the donkey would prick up his long ears. He knew his owner. He knew who was going to feed him that night.

On the contrary, a number of folk today do not have intelligence enough to know that God provides for all their needs. They don't know that God feeds them. They do not even recognize that He exists. What a commentary on this sophisticated generation that no longer needs God. The story is told of a little boy, reared in a Christian home, who was having his first visit away from home. Although he was only going next door for the evening meal, he was eagerly anticipating the experience, and at five o'clock he was dressed and ready to go. When it came time for all of them to sit down at the table, the little fellow, who was accustomed to hearing the giving of thanks at the table, bowed his head and shut his eyes. But the home to which he had been invited was not a Christian home, and they immediately began to pass the food. Because he didn't want to miss anything, he opened his eyes and looked around. The little fellow was just a bit embarrassed, but not having any inhibitions, he raised the question: "Don't you folks thank God for your food?" Then the host was a bit embarrassed but confessed that they did not. The young lad was thoughtful for a moment and then blurted out, "You're exactly like my dog: you just start in."

There are many people like that today. Multitudes of people live just like animals.

God said, "The ox knows his owner, and the donkey his master's crib, but my people do not know." We hear today that man has descended from animals. Who says he has? Man acts like animals act; in fact, it could be said that some animals are smarter than some men. Instead of man descending from animals, maybe animals descended from men; maybe they have evolved into something better than man. Man has dropped pretty low. I think what the Lord said, when He opened up court, reveals that.

He continues His charge in verse 4:

Ah sinful nation, a people laden with iniquity, a seed of evildoers, children that are corrupters: they have forsaken the Lord, they have provoked the Holy One of Israel unto anger, they are gone away backward [Isa. 1:4].

We see God as the Judge of all the earth and of His own people Israel. It seems a strange thing to think of God as a judge, because in the thinking of the world today God has been removed from the throne of judgment. He has been divested of His authority. He has been robbed of His regal prerogatives and shorn of His locks as moral ruler of the universe. He has been driven to the edge of the world and pushed over as excess baggage. Don't think I am being irreverent when I say that modern teaching has given us a warped conception of God. He is characterized as a toothless old man with long whiskers, sitting on the edge of a fleecy cloud with a rainbow around His shoulders. His is simple, senile, and sentimental. He is overwhelmed with mushy love that slops over on every side, dripping honey and tears. He does not have enough courage or backbone to swat a fly or crush a grape. His proper place is in the corner by the fireplace, where He can either crochet or knit. This is the world's conception of God, but that is not how the Bible describes Him. God is going to judge this universe just as He judged His own people. That ought to be a warning not only to nations but also to individuals.

Israel is described as "a people laden with iniquity." This phrase throws a world of light upon the personal invitation that the Lord Jesus gave in the New Testament. He said, "Come unto me, all ye that labour and are heavy laden, and I will give you rest" (Matt. 11:28). Now we know what He meant—"laden with iniquity." The people of Israel were laden with sin. Today His invitation goes out to those who are laden with sin to bring that burden and load to Him and find rest, the rest of redemption.

In this verse God spells out Israel's condition. They are backslidden, they have turned away from God, and they are a people laden with iniquity. Now He is going to spell out in detail the charge that He has made against them.

This brings to mind the philosophy of human government upon which God operates. This system is presented to us in the Book of Judges, and you see this cycle of the history of human government working itself out in the nation. In the Book of Judges we saw Israel serving God, being blessed of God, and prospering. They began, in their prosperity, to turn away from God, and they finally turned to idolatry. They were in rebellion against God; in fact, they forgot Him. Then God delivered them into the hands of the enemy. In a short time they began to cry out to God for deliverance. When they turned to God, He delivered them from their enemies and put them back in the place of blessing. This picture follows all the way through Scripture, and history corroborates the fact that there are three steps in the downfall of any nation. There is religious apostasy, then moral awfulness, and finally political anarchy. Many people don't pay any attention to the cycle until the stage of political anarchy is reached, and then they cry out that the government should be changed and a new system adopted. Well, the problem is not in the government. The problem in Jerusalem was not in the palace, but the problem was within the temple. The trouble begins when there is spiritual apostasy.

Why should ye be stricken any more? ye will revolt more and more: the whole head is sick, and the whole heart faint.

> From the sole of the foot even unto the head there is no
> soundness in it; but wounds, and bruises, and putrify-
> ing sores: they have not been closed, neither bound up,
> neither mollified with ointment.
>
> Your country is desolate, your cities are burned with
> fire: your land, strangers devour it in your presence,
> and it is desolate, as overthrown by strangers [Isa.
> 1:5-7].

What God says in these verses is absolutely true. There is moral awfulness and political anarchy, but God is holding back. This still is not
the charge that He is bringing against them.

> And the daughter of Zion is left as a cottage in a vine-
> yard, as a lodge in a garden of cucumbers, as a besieged
> city.
>
> Except the LORD of hosts had left unto us a very small
> remnant, we should have been as Sodom, and we should
> have been like unto Gomorrah [Isa. 1:8-9].

In other words, if there had not been a faithful remnant, God would
have destroyed Israel as He did Sodom and Gomorrah. But there has
always been a remnant of God's people. There is a remnant today:
there are Christians scattered throughout the world.

> Hear the word of the LORD, ye rulers of Sodom; give ear
> unto the law of our God, ye people of Gomorrah [Isa.
> 1:10].

Now God is spelling it out. The whole problem is spiritual apostasy.

> To what purpose is the multitude of your sacrifices unto
> me? saith the LORD: I am full of the burnt offerings of

rams, and the fat of fed beasts; and I delight not in the blood of bullocks, or of lambs, or of he goats [Isa. 1:11].

God specifies His charges against His people. He has put His hand upon a definite thing, and He is going to prove that particular point in which they are wrong. He puts His finger on the *best* thing in Judah, not the worst. He shows them what is exceedingly wrong. Israel has a God-given religion and a God-appointed ritual in a God-constructed temple, but they are wrong in that which represents the best. They are bringing sacrifices and going through the ritual according to the letter of the Law, but their hearts are in rebellion against God. Their religion is not affecting their conduct. Frankly, that is a problem among believers today. A great many of us have reached the place where we have a form of godliness, but we deny the power thereof.

> **When ye come to appear before me, who hath required this at your hand, to tread my courts?**
>
> **Bring no more vain oblations; incense is an abomination unto me; the new moons and sabbaths, the calling of assemblies, I cannot away with; it is iniquity, even the solemn meeting [Isa. 1:12–13].**

Even doing that which God has commanded becomes wrong when the heart is not in it and when it does not affect the believer's conduct.

If the Lord Jesus were to come into your church next Sunday, would He commend you? Would He compliment you for your faithfulness to Him? Would He tell you how much He appreciates your attendance at the services and your giving to Him? I think not! The One who has "feet as burnished brass," whose "eyes are as a flame of fire," and from whose mouth there goes "a sharp two-edged sword," would not commend us (cf. Prov. 5:4; Dan. 10:6; Rev. 1:14–16). I think He would tell most of us that all of our outward form, all of our lovely testimonies and loud professions, are making Him sick. Would He not tell us that we need to repent and come in humility to Him? Surely this is a warning to the churches of America. Fundamentally, our difficulty today is

spiritual; and, until the professing church repents and has genuine
revival, there is no hope for America.

> **And when ye spread forth your hands, I will hide mine
> eyes from you: yea, when ye make many prayers, I will
> not hear: your hands are full of blood.**
>
> **Wash you, make you clean; put away the evil of your
> doings from before mine eyes; cease to do evil;**
>
> **Learn to do well; seek judgment, relieve the oppressed,
> judge the fatherless, plead for the widow [Isa. 1:15–17].**

God says, "You are nothing in the world but a bunch of phonies. You
come into My presence as if you are really genuine. You go through the
sacrifices, but they have become absolutely meaningless to you." God
has spelled out His charge against them. They are guilty of apostasy.
It has led to moral awfulness and to political anarchy in the nation.
God has called Israel into court and has proved His charge against
them. Israel is like a prisoner standing at the bar waiting for the sentence of judgment. God can now move in to judge them.

But even at this late date God is willing to settle the case out of
court. He says to Israel, "Don't go into court with Me, because you are
going to lose." The Judge has something else to say, and we stand
amazed and aghast at what He says next:

> **Come now, and let us reason together, saith the LORD:
> though your sins be as scarlet, they shall be as white as
> snow; though they be red like crimson, they shall be as
> wool [Isa. 1:18].**

God is saying to Judah, "Do not force Me to render sentence. Settle
your case out of court." In Matthew 5:25 the Lord Jesus said, "Agree
with thine adversary quickly, whiles thou art in the way with him . . ."
—don't wait until he takes you to court. God says that He has a secret

formula, a divine alchemy, a potent prescription, a powerful potion, a heavenly elixir that will take out sin. It is not a secret formula like the newest bomb, but it is more potent. You will find it in Isaiah 53 as the One who was more marred, who suffered more, who died differently, who was wounded for our transgressions. Because He paid the penalty, the Judge is able now to extend mercy to us. The blood of Jesus Christ, God's Son, keeps on cleansing from all sin.

This is God's charge against His people, and this is the basis on which they may turn to Him. If they will turn to Him, He will preserve the nation—He will give them almost one hundred years—then if they don't turn to Him and change their ways, He will send them into captivity.

We see an application of this to our own country. In my beloved country I see political anarchy. It is obvious to most of us that men cannot solve the problems of this nation, and certainly not of the world.

The historical Gibbon gives five reasons for the decline of the Roman Empire in his book, *The Decline and Fall of the Roman Empire*. As the first step towards decline, he lists the undermining of the dignity and the sanctity of the home, which is the basis of human society. The second step includes higher and higher taxes, and the spending of public money for free bread and circuses for the populace. The third was the mad craze for pleasure and sports becoming every year more exciting, more brutal, and more immoral. The fourth step was the building of great armaments when the real enemy was within: the decay of individual responsibility. The fifth was the decay of religion, fading into mere form, losing touch with life, and losing power to guide the people.

You see, a nation's decline begins with spiritual apostasy, which is followed by moral awfulness, and results in political anarchy.

Is there spiritual apostasy in this land of ours? Every informed Christian is aware that modernism has taken over most of the great denominations of America today; and, in this dire day, modernism, by its own confession, has failed. Dr. Reinhold Niebuhr, one of the mouthpieces of liberalism, is quoted as saying that liberal Protestantism has been inclined to sacrifice every characteristic Christian insight if only it could thereby prove itself intellectually respectable, but that liberalism finds itself unable to cope with the tragic experiences of our day.

I find in my file an interesting article clipped from the *Wall Street Journal* several years ago: "What America needs more than railway extension, western irrigation, a low tariff, a bigger cotton crop, and a larger wheat crop is a revival of religion. The kind that father and mother used to have. A religion that counted it good business to take time for family worship each morning right in the middle of wheat harvest. A religion that prompted them to quit work a half hour earlier on Wednesday so that the whole family could get ready to go to prayer meeting." America's problem is the same today; it is a spiritual problem.

Dr. Albert Hyma, when he was professor of history at the University of Michigan in Ann Arbor, said, "The United States of America in the past fifty years has been dominated to a large extent by persons who do not understand the spiritual heritage bequeathed by their own ancestors." Dr. J. Gresham Machen said, "America is coasting downhill on a godly ancestry, and God pity America when we hit the bottom of the hill." Friend, we have hit the bottom of the hill, but God is saying to us, "Come, let us reason together, though your sins be as scarlet, they shall be as white as snow." There is a way out for America, but, if we go the same direction as other nations, our time is limited.

Aaron Burr was a grandson of the great Jonathan Edwards, who, upon an occasion, conducted meetings at Princeton, where Aaron Burr was a student. There was a great spiritual movement in the school. One night Jonathan Edwards preached on the subject, "The Mastery of Jesus." Aaron Burr was deeply stirred, and he went to the room of one of his professors to talk to him about making a decision for Jesus. The professor urged him not to make a decision under any sort of an emotional appeal, but to wait until after the meetings were over. Aaron Burr postponed making a decision and went on to murder a great American and to betray his country. When he was an old man, a young man came to him and said, "Mr. Burr, I want you to meet a Friend of mine." Aaron Burr said, "Who is he?" The young man replied, "He is Jesus Christ, the Savior of my soul." A cold sweat broke out on the forehead of Aaron Burr, and he replied, "Sixty years ago I told God if He would let me alone, I would let Him alone, and He has kept His word!"

There is a way out for America, and there is a way out for you and for me. Someone has stated it this way:

> Philosophy says: Think your way out.
> Indulgence says: Drink your way out.
> Politics says: Spend your way out.
> Science says: Invent your way out.
> Industry says: Work your way out.
> Communism says: Strike your way out.
> Fascism says: Bluff your way out.
> Militarism says: Fight your way out.
> The Bible says: Pray your way out, but
> Jesus Christ says: "I am the way (out)..."

After the Lord brings His charges against Judah and offers them salvation and a way out of their trouble, He continues gently with a warning.

If ye be willing and obedient, ye shall eat the good of the land:

But if ye refuse and rebel, ye shall be devoured with the sword: for the mouth of the LORD hath spoken it [Isa. 1:19–20].

The government of God and the grace of God are two aspects emphasized in the Book of Isaiah. During the remainder of chapter 1 God is attempting to move Judah back to Himself. He is giving the people a warning.

> Therefore saith the Lord, the LORD of hosts, the mighty
> One of Israel, Ah, I will ease me of mine adversaries,
> and avenge me of mine enemies:
>
> And I will turn my hand upon thee, and purely purge
> away thy dross, and take away all thy tin:
>
> And I will restore thy judges as at the first, and thy
> counsellors as at the beginning: afterward thou shalt be
> called, The city of righteousness, the faithful city [Isa.
> 1:24–26].

Judah's destiny depends upon the people's response to God's offer of
forgiving grace. If they are willing to turn from their sin and obey God,
He will bestow His favor upon them materially and spiritually and
protect them from their enemies.

> Zion shall be redeemed with judgment, and her con-
> verts with righteousness.
>
> And the destruction of the transgressors and of the sin-
> ners shall be together, and they that forsake the LORD
> shall be consumed.
>
> For they shall be ashamed of the oaks which ye have
> desired and ye shall be confounded for the gardens that
> ye have chosen [Isa. 1:27–29].

This has to do with idolatry because the idols were placed under the
oak trees, and a garden was planted around them.

> For ye shall be as an oak whose leaf fadeth, and as a
> garden that hath no water.
>
> And the strong shall be as tow, and the maker of it as a
> spark, and they shall both burn together, and none shall
> quench them [Isa. 1:30–31].

God has been misrepresented in the sense that He has been pictured as losing His temper and breaking forth in judgment. That is never a true picture of God. The fact is that our sin is like a wick, and when we play with the spark of sin, the fire will follow. "Be not deceived; God is not mocked: for whatsoever a man soweth, that shall he also reap" (Gal. 6:7).

CHAPTER 2

THEME: Prophecy concerning the last days: the kingdom and the Great Tribulation

Isaiah chapters 2 through 5 constitute one complete prophecy. These chapters look beyond the present time to the last days concerning Israel (the total nation of twelve tribes). As we move through these chapters, God makes it clear that He is speaking of all the tribes of Israel which will be brought back together. God always thinks of Israel as one nation.

The last days of Israel need to be distinguished from the last days of the church. God is not talking about the church in these chapters. There is no way of making what He says applicable to the church. We can be sure of this fact, because in the New Testament Paul says that the church was a mystery which was not revealed in the Old Testament at all. In writing to the Romans, Paul makes this very clear: "Now to him that is of power to stablish you according to my gospel, and the preaching of Jesus Christ, according to the revelation of the mystery, which was kept secret since the world began" (Rom. 16:25). Now if Isaiah had known about the church, it would not have been a new revelation in Paul's day. From Paul's day to the present time the church has been God's agency through which He is giving His message to the world.

However, the church will be removed from the world at the time of the Rapture. Isaiah's message looks beyond the time of the church to the day when God will begin to move in a new way. We call it the Great Tribulation Period, at the close of which He will set·up His kingdom.

PREVIEW OF THE FUTURE FOR JUDAH AND JERUSALEM

The word that Isaiah the son of Amoz saw concerning Judah and Jerusalem [Isa. 2:1].

When Isaiah speaks of Israel, Judah, and Jerusalem, he means exactly these people and places. Judah means Judah, Israel means Israel, and Jerusalem means Jerusalem. If Isaiah uses figures of speech, he will make it perfectly clear that they are figures of speech. The prophet will let you know when he is making a different application. Beware of the fallacy of spiritualizing prophecy in conformity to some outmoded theological cliché which fits into some church's program.

> And it shall come to pass in the last days, that the mountain of the LORD's house shall be established in the top of the mountains, and shall be exalted above the hills; and all nations shall flow unto it [Isa. 2:2].

"It shall come to pass in the last days, that the mountain of the LORD's house shall be established in the top of the mountains." Again let me say that this is not speaking of the last days of the church. The last days of the church pertain to the time of spiritual apostasy. Paul makes this clear in his pastoral epistles of 1 and 2 Timothy: "Now the Spirit speaketh expressly, that in the latter times some shall depart from the faith . . ." (1 Tim. 4:1). You can see that the "latter times" of the church and the "last days" of Israel are not identical, nor are they contemporary, although there is some overlapping. Certainly they do not refer to the same period of time. It is important to note this. The "last days" in this verse refer to the Great Tribulation Period. The Lord Jesus Christ made it clear, when His disciples asked Him, "When shall these things be?" (Luke 21:7 refers to the destruction of Jerusalem) that by the "last days" He meant the Great Tribulation Period. The Great Tribulation ends with the coming of Christ to earth and the setting up of His kingdom. The first section of Isaiah, chapters 2—5, deals with the Great Tribulation Period and the kingdom that shall be set up on this earth.

"The mountain of the LORD's house shall be established in the top of the mountains." This pertains to the nation of Israel after the church has been removed. The word *mountain* in Scripture means "a kingdom, an authority, or a rule." Daniel makes this clear in his prophecy. "The LORD's house shall be established in the top of the mountains"—

that is above all the kingdoms of this earth. The kingdoms of this world shall become the kingdom of the Lord Jesus Christ, and He will be King of Kings and Lord of Lords. One of the reasons that today Israel is such a hot spot and such a sensitive piece of real estate is because it is the very spot that God has chosen to be the political and religious center of the world during the kingdom age. Speaking of those days Daniel says, "Then was the iron, the clay, the brass, the silver, and the gold, broken to pieces together, and became like the chaff of the summer threshingfloors; and the wind carried them away, that no place was found for them: and the stone that smote the image became a great mountain, and filled the whole earth" (Dan. 2:35). God's kingdom will be exalted above the kingdoms of this world.

> **And many people shall go and say, Come ye, and let us go up to the mountain [the kingdom] of the Lord, to the house of the God of Jacob; and he will teach us of his ways, and we will walk in his paths: for out of Zion shall go forth the law, and the word of the Lord from Jerusalem [Isa. 2:3].**

Both government and religion will center in Jerusalem. The Lord Jesus Christ will sit upon the throne of David. One of the primary concerns of those who inhabit the earth will be to discover and do the will of God. They will seek to learn His ways and walk in His paths.

> **And he shall judge among the nations, and shall rebuke many people: and they shall beat their swords into plowshares, and their spears into pruninghooks: nation shall not lift up sword against nation, neither shall they learn war any more [Isa. 2:4].**

"He shall judge among the nations, and shall rebuke many people." The period of the reign of Christ on the earth during the Millennium is another trial period for mankind. And there will be a great many judged during that period; and, of course, multitudes will be saved during that time also.

"They shall beat their swords into plowshares, and their spears into pruninghooks"—the rule of the Lord upon earth at this time will be righteous, and He will compel the nations to practice justice and fairness with each other. For the first time all countries will dwell together in peace. Only during the kingdom age will the people be able to beat their swords into plowshares. Joel 3:10 tells us that during the Tribulation just the opposite will be true: the people will beat their plowshares into swords. In fact, we are living in times like that right now. The idea of disarming nations and disarming individuals is, in my judgment, contrary to the Word of God. In the New Testament the Lord Jesus said, "When a strong man armed keepeth his palace . . ." (Luke 11:21). If you are going to have peace and safety, you must have law and order. The prophecy of beating swords into plowshares will be fulfilled during the Millennium, when the Lord Jesus is reigning. Then you will be able to take the locks off of your doors, and you will be able to walk the streets at night in safety. You will not be drafted, because there will be no more war. There will be no more need for weapons for defense. The kingdom that the Lord is going to establish upon earth will be one of peace. He is the Prince of Peace.

It is futile, nonsensical, and asinine for any man or nation to promise to bring peace upon the earth today. The United Nations, which was founded to help bring peace on earth, is one of the greatest places to carry on battles. It has proven how impotent it is. It cannot bring peace on earth. It has only increased dictatorship on the earth. We do not have peace in the world. If you are a child of God with your thinking cap on and begin to think God's thoughts after Him, you will find that you are living in a big bad, evil world. If you expect to see a brotherhood of all men, you are doomed to disappointment, because man is not capable of bringing peace to this earth. There will be no peace as long as there is sin in the hearts of men and an overweening ambition to rule over other people.

O house of Jacob, come ye, and let us walk in the light of the Lord [Isa. 2:5].

In view of the future that is coming, certainly we should walk in the light of the Lord. This is the only way of peace. When you leave God out, you will never have peace.

> **Therefore thou hast forsaken thy people the house of Jacob, because they be replenished from the east, and are soothsayers like the Philistines, and they please themselves in the children of strangers.**
>
> **Their land also is full of silver and gold, neither is there any end of their treasures; their land is also full of horses, neither is there any end of their chariots:**
>
> **Their land also is full of idols; they worship the work of their own hands, that which their own fingers have made:**
>
> **And the mean man boweth down, and the great man humbleth himself: therefore forgive them not [Isa. 2:6–9].**

Judah adopted new ideas from the heathen and incorporated them into their own religion. They embraced all kinds of ways from Assyria and Babylon. Before long they had joined the rest of the nations in worshipping the creature more than the Creator.

> **Enter into the rock, and hide thee in the dust, for fear of the LORD, and for the glory of his majesty.**
>
> **The lofty looks of man shall be humbled, and the haughtiness of men shall be bowed down, and the LORD alone shall be exalted in that day.**
>
> **For the day of the LORD of hosts shall be upon every one that is proud and lofty, and upon every one that is lifted up; and he shall be brought low [Isa. 2:10–12].**

God intends to break down the proud man—the man who thinks he can rule himself and the man who thinks he can rule the world without God.

> **And upon all the cedars of Lebanon, that are high and lifted up, and upon all the oaks of Bashan [Isa. 2:13].**

The cedars of Lebanon and the oaks of Bashan represent, I believe, the pride of man.

> **And upon all the high mountains, and upon all the hills that are lifted up [Isa. 2:14].**

This has reference to government and society.

> **And upon every high tower, and upon every fenced wall [Isa. 2:15].**

This is a reference to the military, which will be judged.

> **And upon all the ships of Tarshish, and upon all pleasant pictures [Isa. 2:16].**

Commerce and art are going to be judged.

> **And the loftiness of man shall be bowed down, and the haughtiness of men shall be made low: and the LORD alone shall be exalted in that day [Isa. 2:17].**

God is going to put down all of the pride and pomp of men.

> **And the idols he shall utterly abolish [Isa. 2:18].**

God is going to get rid of all false religion.

> **And they shall go into the holes of the rocks, and into the caves of the earth, for the fear of the LORD, and for the glory of his majesty, when he ariseth to shake terribly the earth [Isa. 2:19].**

The Book of Revelation repeats what man will do in that day of judgment: "And the kings of the earth, and the great men, and the rich men, and the chief captains, and the mighty men, and every bondman, and every free man, hid themselves in the dens and in the rocks of the mountains; And said to the mountains and rocks, Fall on us, and hide us from the face of him that sitteth on the throne, and from the wrath of the Lamb" (Rev. 6:15–16).

All you see on television today has to do with the political economy, government, commerce, art, the pomp and pride of man—and the religion of man. The day is coming when all of man's pride is going to be brought low, and the Lord Jesus Christ will be *exalted* on earth. Today He is not being given His proper place in government, in society, in business, in art, or in the pomp and ceremony of the world—or even in the religion of the world. He is left out today. When He comes again, men are going to run for the caves of the earth. I don't know whether men were ever cavemen or not, but a day is coming in the future when men are going back to the caves.

> **In that day a man shall cast his idols of silver, and his idols of gold, which they made each one for himself to worship, to the moles and to the bats;**
>
> **To go into the clefts of the rocks, and into the tops of the ragged rocks, for fear of the Lord, and for the glory of his majesty, when he ariseth to shake terribly the earth [Isa. 2:20–21].**

"When he ariseth to shake terribly the earth" is the time of the Great Tribulation.

> **Cease ye from man, whose breath is in his nostrils: for wherein is he to be accounted of? [Isa. 2:22].**

Don't put your confidence in man. You and I exhale, but we don't know whether we are going to inhale the next breath. That is the frailty of man—if he misses one breath he is out of the picture. Multitudes today going about their daily business will have fatal heart attacks and disappear from the earth's scene. Don't put your confidence in man. Put your confidence in the Lord Jesus Christ today.

CHAPTER 3

THEME: The cause of Israel's undoing: weak government; loose and low morals

This is a continuation of the prophecy begun in chapter 2 (chs. 2—5 constitute a complete prophecy). In this section on judgment, chapter 3 reveals God's judgment leveled particularly against the nation of Israel. Although it has application to other nations, the interpretation is definitely to Israel. Further along in this judgment section we will see God's judgment of surrounding nations, which are among the most remarkable prophecies in the Word of God, and many of them have been literally fulfilled. However, we find that God's judgment against Israel is more severe and intense than against any other nation. Why? Well, Israel was the nation God had chosen in a peculiar way, and it enjoyed a particularly close relationship to God. Privilege creates responsibility.

Because privilege always creates responsibility, I believe God will judge the Untied States more severely than He will judge any of our contemporary nations—like China, for example. The United States has been privileged to know the Word of God as no other nation has—except Israel.

Israel as a nation had more light than any of its neighbors, and light rejected brings severe punishment, as will be illustrated in this book.

The subject of God's judgment may be offensive to you, but please don't hide your head in the sand like the proverbial ostrich. Let's face reality whether we like it or not. God does judge sin. Not only will He judge sin in the future, He has judged it in the past. And he makes no apology for it.

The prophecy before us is a picture of Isaiah's day, and it has been fulfilled. However, its fulfillment does not exhaust its meaning, because the condition described will prevail again at the end times and will bring down the wrath of God in judgment—not only upon Israel but also upon the nations of the world.

The first fifteen verses deal with the subject of weak government and women's dress. These seem to be totally unrelated subjects, but we shall see that they are not as far removed as they appear to be. Weak government is caused by a lack of leadership, as evidenced by women rulers—and we will see what he means by this.

WEAK GOVERNMENT

For, behold, the Lord, the Lᴏʀᴅ of hosts, doth take away from Jerusalem and from Judah the stay and the staff, the whole stay of bread, and the whole stay of water [Isa. 3:1].

This verse confines us to Jerusalem and Judah.

Although man does not live by bread alone, he surely needs it. This famine is a judgment of God. There are thirteen famines mentioned in the Word of God, and every one of them is a judgment from Him upon the nation of Israel.

The mighty man, and the man of war, the judge, and the prophet, and the prudent, and the ancient,

The captain of fifty, and the honourable man, and the counsellor, and the cunning artificer, and the eloquent orator [Isa. 3:2–3].

God is going to remove not only bread and water but all the men of leadership. Qualified men for high positions are lacking, and this is a judgment from God.

This can be brought up to date. Have you been impressed by the fact that there are no great men on the contemporary scene? There are quite a few men who are passing themselves off as great, but they would have been pygmies in the days of Washington, Lincoln, Jackson, Teddy Roosevelt, or the men who wrote the Declaration of Independence. I am not taking sides with any political party when I say this, but today there are many ambitious men, young and old alike, who have practically no qualifications as statesmen. One hundred years ago they would have been called cheap politicians, but today they are called statesmen!

We have men of war, but we have no great generals. Our army would not be in the situation it is in today if it had strong leadership. There is lack of leadership in our judicial system. We have an alarming crime wave because we have pygmies sitting in the seats of judgment. Where is the prophet, the prudent, and the ancient? We have no statesmen at all today. What we have is a group of clever politicians who know how to compromise. I am not talking about a certain political party. I am simply saying that it is always the mark of a decadent age and the judgment of God when a nation is not producing great men.

Moving into the field of the arts—what greatness do you see on the television screen? I get rather bored with the television talk programs. Generally the master of ceremonies comes out and says, "I am going to introduce you to a great artist, a genius." And some little peanut comes out on stage, strums a guitar—doesn't play any music at all—just yells at the top of his voice. And he is hailed as a genius! Another man comes along who is introduced as a great literary light, and all that he has written is a dirty book. My friend, we lack greatness in this day, but we are not willing to admit it because we have become a proud nation.

Where is greatness in the field of education? We used to believe that the educators had the solution to the problems of the world. Today it is obvious that educators cannot control even their own campuses.

It is said that we used to have wooden ships and iron men, but now we have iron ships and wooden men. I would go further than that and call them paper doll men. Our leadership is just a string of paper dolls!

And I will give children to be their princes, and babes shall rule over them [Isa. 3:4].

As far as ability is concerned, men in high positions today should be wearing diapers. Juvenile adults are our rulers, and they are totally incompetent. That is exactly what brought Israel down to ruin in that day. Their leaders had the mental level of children, and God sent them into captivity. He judged them.

> **And the people shall be oppressed, every one by another, and every one by his neighbour: the child shall behave himself proudly against the ancient, and the base against the honourable [Isa. 3:5].**

My friend, it sounds as if Isaiah were talking about our day, but the same was true in his day. The child, the little college student, is saying, "Listen to me. I have something to say." I have been listening to them for years, and I haven't heard them say anything yet. One class is set against another class. "The people shall be oppressed, every one by another." We have groups of minorities who want to inflict their ways on others. Christians are a minority also, but certainly we are not being heard.

> **For Jerusalem is ruined, and Judah is fallen: because their tongue and their doings are against the LORD, to provoke the eyes of his glory [Isa. 3:8].**

"Jerusalem is ruined, and Judah is fallen"—that's what the prophet says. We don't have many of God's men in our day standing up, pointing at our nation, and saying, "Our cities are ruined," although it is as true as it was in Isaiah's time.

"Because their tongue and their doings are against the LORD, to provoke the eyes of his glory." This is the key to the chapter, and it is the key to the ruin of Israel and of any other nation. God judges nations by their relationship to Him.

The problem with the United States of America is that God has been run out of Washington, D.C. God has been ruled out in every area of our lives. A few little men think they can rule the world. How we need to be humbled, and I think we have been humbled. Russia has humbled us. China has humbled us. And little Vietnam humbled us.

We are being humbled all over the world; yet we don't wake up. We continue merrily on our way, coasting downhill on our godly ancestry.

The shew of their countenance doth witness against them; and they declare their sin as Sodom, they hide it not. Woe unto their soul! for they have rewarded evil unto themselves [Isa. 3:9].

Sin is out in the open. What used to be done in the backyard has been moved to the front yard. What was done under cover, is now done in the open. The boast is that we are more honest now. No, we're not more honest; we are the same hypocrites that our fathers were. They were hypocrites because they hid their sin, and we are hypocrites because we are sinning out in the open and trying to say that the sin is good! This is exactly what Israel was saying.

Say ye to the righteous, that it shall be well with him: for they shall eat the fruit of their doings [Isa. 3:10].

God promises to deliver His own people.

Woe unto the wicked! it shall be ill with him: for the reward of his hands shall be given him [Isa. 3:11].

This is another way of saying, "Whatsoever a man sows, that shall he also reap."

As for my people, children are their oppressors, and women rule over them. O my people, they which lead thee cause thee to err, and destroy the way of thy paths [Isa. 3:12].

"Children are their oppressors." The greatest problem in our day is juvenile delinquency. The greatest increase in crime is among young people, and the age drops every year.

"Women rule over them." Oh, "women's lib" will not like Isaiah, and they won't like me any better. "O my people, they which lead thee cause thee to err, and destroy the way of thy paths." Whether women rulers are meant here or effeminate men is not clear. I think it is a little of both. The women's liberation movement is another sign of a decadent age. When women act like men, they are not coming up to a high level but are descending to the male level. The woman has been given a greater amount of tenderness, but when she becomes as blase and brutal as a man, she actually becomes worse than he is. And that is the downfall of the nation. That was true in Israel's case, and it will be true in our own nation. Go to Italy and see the ruins of Pompeii, and then consider what removed the Romans from the earthly scene. The nation that once ruled the world collapsed—not because they were attacked by someone on the outside, but because they fell from within.

Listen to Him now as He pleads with His people:

The Lord standeth up to plead, and standeth to judge the people.

The Lord will enter into judgment with the ancients of his people, and the princes thereof: for ye have eaten up the vineyard; the spoil of the poor is in your houses [Isa. 3:13–14].

"The ancients" and "the princes" are the leaders of the nation. God lays the blame on the adult leadership. The juvenile problem did not originate with young people.

In Isaiah's time there were a few who were trying to get rich and rule over everyone else. "The spoil of the poor is in your houses." Godless capitalism and godless labor are big problems in our nation, and one is as bad as the other. The whole difficulty is that we are away from God. God is standing up ready to plead or ready to judge, and He will let the nation determine which it will be. We can have it either way. He will do one or the other.

WOMEN'S DRESS

Moreover the Lord saith, Because the daughters of Zion are haughty, and walk with stretched forth necks and

wanton eyes, walking and mincing as they go, and making a tinkling with their feet [Isa. 3:16].

What a picture of womanhood! The problem, of course, is in the heart. In 1 Peter 3:1–4 we read, "Likewise, ye wives, be in subjection to your own husbands; that, if any obey not the word, they also may without the word be won by the conversation of the wives; While they behold your chaste conversation [or, conduct] coupled with fear. [This doesn't mean that she is to take abuse from him, but she is to live a godly life before him.] Whose adorning let it not be that outward adorning of plaiting the hair, and of wearing of gold, or of putting on of apparel; [if you are trying to hold your husband with sex, you'll lose him]. But let it be the hidden man of the heart, in that which is not corruptible, even the ornament of a meek and quiet spirit, which is in the sight of God of great price."

When I counsel with young couples I always tell them that there are three cords that hold marriage together, and a threefold cord is not easily broken. There is the physical cord, and that is important. Also there is the psychological cord—the same interests. Third, there is the spiritual cord—the same love for God and His work. If a wife is trying to hold her husband with only her physical attraction, the time will come when he is no longer interested. This is what Peter is saying. A wife's attraction should be more than the way she dresses and styles her hair. Her beauty should be in the way she lives her life with a gentle and quiet spirit.

Isaiah pictures the women of his day as haughty and sexy, "mincing as they go, and making a tinkling with their feet."

Therefore the Lord will smite with a scab the crown of the head of the daughters of Zion, and the LORD will discover their secret parts [Isa. 3:17].

He is talking about a disease. Do you know that there is an epidemic of venereal disease in our nation right now? So many of our young girls look appealing, but they are like serpents along the way, as many a man is finding out to his sorrow.

In that day the Lord will take away the bravery of their tinkling ornaments about their feet, and their cauls, and their round tires like the moon.

The chains, and the bracelets, and the mufflers,

The bonnets, and the ornaments of the legs, and the headbands, and the tablets, and the earrings,

The rings, and nose jewels,

The changeable suits of apparel, and the mantles, and the wimples, and the crisping pins,

The glasses, and the fine linen, and the hoods, and the veils.

And it shall come to pass, that instead of sweet smell there shall be stink; and instead of a girdle a rent; and instead of well set hair baldness; and instead of a stomacher a girding of sackcloth; and burning instead of beauty [Isa. 3:18–24].

Women's dress is the barometer of any civilization. When women's dress is modest it tells something about the nation as a whole.

In these last few verses twenty articles of women's wear are mentioned by name. There certainly is nothing wrong with a woman dressing in style—if the style is not immodest. I feel that all of us should look the best we can with what we have, even though some of us don't have too much to work with. God is not condemning the women of Israel for dressing in the style of their day. He is talking about the inner life. They were haughty and brazen. Real adornment is beneath the skin, not from the skin outward. Women's dress is the key to a nation's morals.

Thy men shall fall by the sword, and thy mighty in the war.

And her gates shall lament and mourn; and she being desolate shall sit upon the ground [Isa. 3:25–26].

There was a Roman medal which showed a woman weeping; the insignia beneath her read, *Judea capta*. It represented the captives of Israel. Because Israel did not heed the warnings God gave them, they went into captivity.

As I write this, the terrible loss of our young men in Vietnam is still fresh in our minds. Now we are a nation at peace, and we feel very comfortable. But, my friend, the bombs are yet to fall on our nation, which I believe will be God's judgment upon us.

CHAPTER 4

THEME: Conditions that did prevail during the Babylonian captivity and will prevail at the establishment of the kingdom

This chapter is a continuation of one complete prophecy which began in chapter 2 and will conclude in chapter 5. In these chapters we actually have a synopsis of the entire Book of Isaiah, because he touches all the bases here that he will touch upon in the rest of the book.

Chapter 4 is the briefest chapter in the book; it is only six verses long. We have set before us a description of the conditions which prevailed at the time of the Babylonian captivity and also of the conditions which will exist during the Great Tribulation Period right before the setting up of the messianic kingdom.

The structure of the chapter is very simple. The first verse is the only one that depicts conditions during the time of the Great Tribulation, or the last days. The remainder of the chapter sets before the reader the preparation that will be necessary for entering the kingdom. This section, of course, is entirely anticipatory.

And in that day seven women shall take hold of one man, saying, We will eat our own bread, and wear our own apparel: only let us be called by thy name, to take away our reproach [Isa. 4:1].

These conditions will prevail because of the frightening casualties of war. That has been true of all wars, and these conditions will exist in the time of the Great Tribulation. In other words, because the man-power population will be so decimated by war, there will be a surplus of women, so much so that seven women will be willing to share one man in that day! And all of them will be willing to hold down a job. I suppose a man will do nothing in the world but keep books for the women and make sure that they turn in their proper share. It is an awful condition that will prevail. After World War II we experienced, to an extent, a manpower shortage in this country and also following our involvement in the Vietnam war. At that time, when I heard that there was something like a surplus of 80,000 women, I kidded my wife that she had better take good care of me as there just weren't enough men to go around!

> **In that day shall the branch of the LORD be beautiful and glorious, and the fruit of the earth shall be excellent and comely for them that are escaped of Israel [Isa. 4:2].**

"In that day" refers to the Day of the Lord. This phrase will occur again and again in Isaiah (and in all the prophets), and it will be mentioned in the New Testament. Joel particularly will have something to say about it. It begins as every Hebrew day always begins—at sundown. It begins with darkness and moves to the dawn. It begins with the Great Tribulation and goes on into the millennial kingdom.

There is also a reference in this verse to the Lord Jesus Christ for He is "the branch." There are eighteen Hebrew words translated by the one English word *branch*. All of them refer to the Lord Jesus. In this verse the word *branch* means "sprout." Later, we are going to be told that he is a branch out of a dry ground. He is something green that has sprung up in the desert.

> **And it shall come to pass, that he that is left in Zion, and he that remaineth in Jerusalem, shall be called holy, even every one that is written among the living in Jerusalem [Isa. 4:3].**

There will be those of God's people, both of Israel and the Gentiles, during the Great Tribulation, who will survive that period. (Those who are martyred will, of course, be resurrected at the end of that time.) In Matthew the Lord Jesus expressed it in a way that may seem strange, but He is looking at the end of Tribulation when He says, ". . . he that shall endure unto the end, the same shall be saved" (Matt.

24:13). Well, they were *sealed* at the beginning to make sure they got through it. The Shepherd is able to keep His own sheep, and therefore they are going to endure unto the end. We have the same thought in Revelation 7 which speaks of that great company, both Jew and Gentile, who were sealed at the beginning of the Great Tribulation and came through that period.

> **When the Lord shall have washed away the filth of the daughters of Zion, and shall have purged the blood of Jerusalem from the midst thereof by the spirit of judgment, and by the spirit of burning [Isa. 4:4].**

Zechariah 13:1 tells us, "In that day there shall be a fountain opened to the house of David and to the inhabitants of Jerusalem for sin and for uncleanness."

God's people must be *prepared* to enter the kingdom. This brings up a very pertinent question. Each year as we stand on the threshold of a new year, we say we are going to do better. We have been saying the same thing for years. My question is, "Are you fit today for heaven?" Suppose God took you to heaven as you are right now. Would you be fit for heaven? I cannot answer this question for you, but God is going to have to do a great deal of repair work on Vernon McGee to make him ready for heaven. That is what life is all about: it is a school to prepare us for eternity. Many people make a sad mistake to think that this life is all there is. Preparation is made on earth for *eternity*. Suppose God took you to heaven as you are, would you be a square peg in a round hole? I am afraid I would be. Beloved, it does not yet appear what we shall be. He is going to have to make some changes.

> **And the LORD will create upon every dwelling place of mount Zion, and upon her assemblies, a cloud and smoke by day, and the shining of a flaming fire by night: for upon all the glory shall be a defence [Isa. 4:5].**

The glory of God will be upon every house in the kingdom, not just upon the temple. What a glorious thing that will be!

And there shall be a tabernacle for a shadow in the daytime from the heat, and for a place of refuge, and for a covert from storm and from rain [Isa. 4:6].

Security will come to the nation Israel in that day—at last. Today Israel does not have peace. Therefore this prophecy is not being fulfilled. The Jews are not back in the land with every man dwelling under his vine and fig tree in peace.

Note that peace always follows grace, mercy, and cleansing. The problem has never been with a political party. The real problem has never been with a foreign country. The problem is in the human heart. We war because it is in our hearts. Man is a warlike creature because he is a sinner and he refuses to deal with that question. There will be one war right after the other until the heart of man is changed.

CHAPTER 5

THEME: The song of the vineyard; the six woes that follow

This chapter brings us to the end of the section which was begun in chapter 2. The first seven verses are the song of the vineyard which tells of the sins of the nation Israel and the coming captivity. The balance of the chapter gives the six woes or the six specific sins which bring down the judgment of God upon the nation. The penalty for each sin is listed.

THE SONG OF THE VINEYARD

Those who can read the song of the vineyard in Hebrew tell me that it is without doubt one of the most beautiful songs that has ever been written. There is nothing quite like it; there is nothing to rival it. It is a musical symphony, and it is absolutely impossible to reproduce in English. It is truly a song and comparable to any of the psalms.

The vineyard is the house of Israel (v. 7). Thus, the vineyard becomes one of the two figures in Scripture that is taken from the botanical world to represent the whole nation of Israel. The fig tree is the other figure that is used.

Before His death our Lord gave a parable of the vineyard which obviously referred to the whole house of Israel (see Matt. 21:33–46). In Isaiah the prophet announces the imminent captivity of the northern kingdom into Assyria and of the southern kingdom into Babylon. In Matthew the Lord Jesus Christ showed that God had given Israel a second chance in their return from the seventy-year Babylonian captivity, but the nation's rejection of the Son of God would usher in a more extensive and serious dispersion.

Now listen to the song of the vineyard:

Now will I sing to my wellbeloved a song of my beloved touching his vineyard. My wellbeloved hath a vineyard in a very fruitful hill [Isa. 5:1].

"My beloved" is the Lord Jesus Christ. He is the Messiah of Israel and the Savior of the world.

"A very fruitful hill"—there is nothing wrong with the soil. The problem is with the vineyard itself, that is, with the vine. Verse 7 makes it quite clear that the vineyard is the house of Israel; it is Judah. It is not the church or something else. This is clear; we do not have to guess at these things.

God is again inviting us into court to consider His charges against Israel. And, my friend, the minute you listen to Him and to His charge against Israel, you will find yourself condemned.

And he fenced it, and gathered out the stones thereof, and planted it with the choicest vine, and built a tower in the midst of it, and also made a winepress therein: and he looked that it should bring forth grapes, and it brought forth wild grapes [Isa. 5:2].

God took the nation Israel out of Egypt and placed them in the Promised Land. He expected them to produce the fruits of righteousness and required them to glorify His name. They failed ignominiously.

And now, O inhabitants of Jerusalem, and men of Judah, judge, I pray you, betwixt me and my vineyard [Isa. 5:3].

God asks these people to judge, to equate the difference between God and Israel. Very candidly, friend, when you look at your own life are you ready to complain against God? I know how I whined and howled when I got cancer. I thought the Lord was being unfair. Then I had the opportunity of lying alone on that hospital bed and looking at my life. My friend, God wasn't wrong—*I* was wrong and I needed to face up to it. We need to get rid of the idea that somehow we are something special. God is not going to do anything to us that is unjust. He is not going to do anything that is wrong. You and I are wrong; God isn't wrong.

> **What could have been done more to my vineyard, that I have not done in it? wherefore, when I looked that it should bring forth grapes, brought it forth wild grapes? [Isa. 5:4].**

God states that He made every provision on His part for them to produce the fruits of righteousness. Their failure under these circumstances becomes serious indeed.

> **And now go to; I will tell you what I will do to my vineyard: I will take away the hedge thereof, and it shall be eaten up; and break down the wall thereof, and it shall be trodden down:**

> **And I will lay it waste: it shall not be pruned, nor digged; but there shall come up briers and thorns: I will also command the clouds that they rain no rain upon it [Isa. 5:5–6].**

This is a clear prediction of the forthcoming captivities of both the kingdoms. For over five hundred years God had kept the great nations of the world off the land bridge of three continents—Palestine. He put a wall around the children of Israel. God would not let anybody touch them, though many times He could have judged them. But God says, "You are my vineyard. I have hedged you in, but now I am breaking down the wall." First Syria, then Assyria, then Babylon—they all poured into Israel's land and laid it waste. And in spite of everything that has been done in that land today, it is still a pretty desolate looking place. God has judged it.

"I will also command the clouds that they rain no rain upon it." For over a thousand years, the former (fall) and the latter (spring) rains did not fall. That is why that land is so desolate today. The former rains, I understand, have begun, but not the latter.

> For the vineyard of the LORD of hosts is the house of Is-
> rael, and the men of Judah his pleasant plant: and he
> looked for judgment, but behold oppression; for righ-
> teousness, but behold a cry [Isa. 5:7].

You don't have to guess whom the prophet is talking about. The vineyard refers to the whole house of Israel, and this verse makes that crystal clear. And in that vineyard God "looked for judgment, but behold
oppression; for righteousness, but behold a cry."

THE SIX WOES

Once again God is going to spell it all out. Six woes are mentioned
here, and each one tells of a certain sin for which God is judging Israel. If you want to apply these to your life or to the life of our nation,
you can do it. But the interpretation is for Israel; it has already been
fulfilled for them. We can certainly make application to our own
hearts and lives, however.

> Woe unto them that join house to house, that lay field to
> field, till there be no place, that they may be placed
> alone in the midst of the earth! [Isa. 5:8].

This is the first sin of Israel. What is it? This sin is the lust of the eye;
more specifically, it is covetousness. Colossians 3:5 tells us: "Mortify
therefore your members which are upon the earth; fornication, uncleanness, inordinate affection, evil concupiscence, and covetousness, which is idolatry." Covetousness is idolatry. It is a big business
expanding at the expense of the little man. That is what happened in
Israel—the little man was squeezed out. It was done so that great for-
tunes might be accumulated. The only excuse for such expansion is
the insatiable greed for more property and possessions. God will
judge the people for that.

   It is a sad story that we have here. The picture is one of a great
complex of farms. In Isaiah's day the people were agricultural people.
They built big corporations, big complexes. This was not done for the

good of the little man, the small operator. It was done to accumulate wealth. Anything to which you give yourself completely becomes your religion. Many people today are worshipping at the altar of covetousness.

Covetousness is a mean-looking god. It has the face of a silver dollar or a dollar bill. It is one thing that brought down Israel and for which God judged them. Instead of following God's instructions, they were beginning to take all of the richness from the soil. We are doing the same thing today. We are living in a world which is actually depleted of its energy. We are frantically searching for oil, for any kind of energy that can be used. Why? Because men are covetous, and that covetousness is depleting the earth of its riches. That is a judgment of God.

> **In mine ears said the LORD of hosts, Of a truth many houses shall be desolate, even great and fair, without inhabitant.**

> **Yea, ten acres of vineyard shall yield one bath, and the seed of an homer shall yield an ephah [Isa. 5:9–10].**

God is simply saying that even though they expand their lands, the yield will not be great because there will be a famine which will decimate the crop. Extended holdings will not produce a bumper crop at all.

The earth you and I are living on is running short of energy. We are running out of oil. We are running out of arable lands. This subject of ecology is an important matter. Pollution is destroying much of the earth. One of these days we are going to be on a desolate planet. We are quickly running out of energy. If you are planning on taking a trip, you had better go now, because there is going to be a shortage of fuel. It may not happen in our lifetime, but there are those who believe that it will be in our lifetime. This is the judgment that God made on the nation Israel in that day.

> **Woe unto them that rise up early in the morning, that they may follow strong drink; that continue until night, till wine inflame them!**

**And the harp, and the viol, the tabret, and pipe, and
wine, are in their feasts: but they regard not the work of
the LORD, neither consider the operation of his hands
[Isa. 5:11–12].**

This is the second woe, the second sin. Drunkenness and pleasure on
a national scale are the sins mentioned here, and they lead to the dead-
ening of all spiritual perception.

I notice that the news media do not release today, as they did a
number of years ago, the number of alcoholics that we have in this
country. The last report I got, which was several years ago, was that
there were ten million alcoholics in the United States. They *do* put in
the paper what is done with the tax money the liquor industry pays. It
goes to take care of the alcoholics and to maintain police forces who
take care of the accidents caused by drunk drivers! Of course, no one
can pay for the lives of the innocent victims taken in such useless accidents. No one knows how many decisions are made in our government
by people who have just come from a cocktail party. These are the
things that lower the morals of a nation. They destroy a nation and eat
at its vitals like a cancer. Such a nation is on the verge of falling prey to
an enemy without.

**Therefore my people are gone into captivity, because
they have no knowledge: and their honorable men are
famished, and their multitude dried up with thirst [Isa.
5:13].**

The majority of the people in this country think it is rather sophisticated to drink, that it is the thing to do. I was very much interested in
an article in which the man being interviewed was the director of a
therapeutic community for drug addicts in New York. One of the ques-
tions he was asked was, "Is there anything parents can do to prevent
children from turning to drugs?" This man, whose answers indicated
that he probably was not a Christian, said that of paramount importance is an attitude in the home of not using drugs, pills, or alcohol as
a means of solving life's problems. He went on to say that he didn't

mean that taking an occasional social drink was taboo (of course, he would not go so far as to say that!), but that the old rule, "Monkey see, monkey do," is just as valid on this issue as it is on any other. He said that youngsters who grow up in an atmosphere of drug abuse will be among the first to try marijuana or pills when confronted with their own problems.

Father, mother, if you continue to drink cocktails—and I see it in many restaurants as I travel across the country—don't be surprised if your Willie or Mary gets on dope. They will probably move in that direction. After all, why do you drink? The problem of young people on drugs started in the home where parents drink in order to face life. That is what destroys the home and the nation. Drunkenness is one of the things that brought down Israel. What about our nation?

> **Therefore hell hath enlarged herself, and opened her mouth without measure: and their glory, and their multitude, and their pomp, and he that rejoiceth, shall descend into it [Isa. 5:14].**

The word translated "hell" in this verse is actually "the grave." It is not a reference to the lake of fire as we think of hell today. It is the Hebrew word *sheol*. It means that "the grave demands." You find this same word in Proverbs 30:16 which says, "The grave; and the barren womb; the earth that is not filled with water; and the fire that saith not, It is enough." Death, or the grave, (both satisfactory translations of *sheol*) is never satisfied. This is the question to ask when you stand at the grave of someone: Where is he? Job asked this question, "But man dieth, and wasteth away: yea, man giveth up the ghost, and where is he?" (Job 14:10). That is the question everybody is going to have to ask.

Hell at first did not have the idea of a locality, but in time it was thought that since God was in heaven or above, hell or the grave must be below or down. In the New Testament the word *hades* is the same as the Old Testament *sheol*. The Lord Jesus used this word when He said, "And thou, Capernaum, which art exalted unto heaven, shalt be brought down to hell [hades] . . ." (Matt. 11:23). The Lord was not talking about a literal descent into the heart of the earth. He simply meant that Capernaum was going to be brought down, and all you have to do is look at the ruins of that place today to know that what He said was true. We always attach strong moral connotations to the terms of direction, up and *down*: up towards God and down towards hell. Here Isaiah is saying that the nation of Israel will be brought down. They are going to be taken into captivity, they are going to be brought down to the grave, and the glory of the nation will be turned into dust because of her drunkenness and pleasure.

Rudyard Kipling was a prophet as well as a poet when he wrote in his "Recessional":

> "Lo, all our pomp of yesterday
> Is one with Nineveh and Tyre."

Woe unto them that draw iniquity with cords of vanity, and sin as it were with a cart rope [Isa. 5:18].

This can be translated: "Woe to those whose wickedness is helped by words of lying, who in their pride and unbelief the wrath of God define." You can make a poem out of it, you see. This is the third woe, or the third sin. This is the picture of a nation giving itself in abandon to sin without shame or conscience.

That say, Let him make speed, and hasten his work, that we may see it: and let the counsel of the Holy One of Israel draw nigh and come, that we may know it! [Isa. 5:19].

In other words, they challenge God to do anything about their sin. It is interesting to note that no penalty is mentioned. The very silence here is frightening: the penalty is too awful to mention. The history of the deportation of the nation to Babylon tells something of the frightful judgment of God upon a people who sin with impunity against Him and defy Him. God will judge them.

Do you remember Psalm 137? In that psalm Israel prayed against Babylon. They prayed that there would be an eye for an eye and a tooth for a tooth. They said, "Happy shall he be, that taketh and dasheth thy little ones against the stones" (Ps. 137:9). That is horrible beyond words, but that is the judgment that came to Israel. My friend, God is a God of love, but when you reach the place where you defy Him and turn your back on Him, there is no hope for you. Judgment comes. There are just too many instances in history to deny this fact, unless you want to shut your eyes to them.

Woe unto them that call evil good, and good evil; that put darkness for light, and light for darkness; that put bitter for sweet, and sweet for bitter! [Isa. 5:20].

This is the fourth sin against which the fourth woe is leveled. It is an attempt to destroy God's standards of right and wrong by substituting man's values which contradict His moral standards. This is the confusion that comes upon a nation when they abandon God after He has blessed them in the past for their acknowledgment of Him. England is a present-day example of this, and America is fast deteriorating in the same direction.

We have this confusion in our standards of marriage today. I listened to a very beautiful little girl tell her story on a television interview program. She was living with a man to whom she was not married, and the reason she gave was that she was being honest—she did not believe in being a hypocrite. I have news for her: she is not only a hypocrite and dishonest, she knows that what she is doing is wrong and that she should be married. God says she is living in adultery. I don't care, my friend, what you might think about it—that's what God says.

Woe unto them that are wise in their own eyes, and prudent in their own sight! [Isa. 5:21].

This is the fifth woe, the sin of pride. God hates this above all else. Proverbs 6:16–17 tells us, "These six things doth the LORD hate: yea, seven are an abomination unto him: A proud look, a lying tongue, and hands that shed innocent blood." Pride was the sin of Satan according to 1 Timothy 3:6, "Not a novice, lest being lifted up with pride he fall into the condemnation of the devil." Pride is number one on God's hate parade.

> **Woe unto them that are mighty to drink wine, and men of strength to mingle strong drink:**
>
> **Which justify the wicked for reward, and take away the righteousness of the righteous from him! [Isa. 5:22-23].**

This is the sixth and last woe. Here a people have become so sodden with drunkenness that they have lost their sense of justice. Injustice and crookedness prevail, and the righteous man is falsely accused. No nation can long survive which drops so low in morals that it loses its sense of values.

Ours is a day when people are saying that wrong is right and right is wrong. In my younger days I was in a little theater group, and I remember memorizing a line from *The Great Divide:* "Wrong is wrong from the moment it happens 'til the crack of doom, and all the angels in heaven working overtime cannot make it different or less by a hair." My friend, wrong is still wrong.

> **Therefore as the fire devoureth the stubble, and the flame consumeth the chaff, so their root shall be as rottenness, and their blossom shall go up as dust: because they have cast away the law of the LORD of hosts, and despised the word of the Holy One of Israel [Isa. 5:24].**

"As the fire devoureth the stubble." Though the process of deterioration and rottenness is slow and unobserved, the penalty comes like a fire in the stubble. It is fast and furious and cannot be deterred. It is the anger of the Lord bursting forth in judgment. It moves the frightful judgment of God in the last days.

In Matthew 12:20 the Lord Jesus Christ said, "A bruised reed shall he not break, and smoking flax shall he not quench, till he send forth judgment unto victory." He was quoting from Isaiah 42:3. There are certain sins that bring their own judgment; drunkenness is one, and drug abuse is another. I could give many instances of men I have seen engaged in these sins, and the sin worked in their own lives, in the lives of their families, and in their bodies until it destroyed them. God didn't have to do a thing. The smoking flax *will* break into flame, and that bruised reed *will* die. The very sin that we commit is the sin that will destroy us.

When I was a young man in Nashville, Tennessee, I went to a dentist who was also a good friend. One day he told me something which had happened in that town several years before. He told me that one of the most reputable doctors in the city had headed up a dope ring. It was difficult for the law to reach him because of his position. One day the doctor tightened up on the dope in order to get a higher price. For a brief period of time he cut off the supply of dope. This, of course, pushed the price up higher. During that time both his son and daughter were exposed as addicts. He knew nothing about their problem until he cut off the dope supply. That man had the shock of his life, and it apparently led to his death, which occurred shortly afterward. God doesn't have to put His hand in and judge every time. In many instances He just lets sin take its course.

The sin of drinking is all around us today. God doesn't do anything about it. He doesn't have to. Drunkenness will bring its own judgment. Judgment will come to the individual, and it will come to the nation. Those of us who have been in the ministry for a long time have seen drinking increase through the years, and I have seen some heavy drinkers be converted and turn to the Lord. But some of them would leave a bottle in the icebox, just in case. That is what leads many back into the awful sin of drinking. That is what Paul is talking about in Romans 8:12 when he says, "Therefore, brethren, we are debtors, not to the flesh, to live after the flesh." In other words, make no arrangements with the flesh to do what it wants to do. Don't leave a bottle in the refrigerator. Take the bottle out and break it. Many of us kid ourselves about our sins, but some of these sins touch all of us, I am sure.

Therefore is the anger of the Lord kindled against his people, and he hath stretched forth his hand against

**them, and hath smitten them: and the hills did tremble,
and their carcases were torn in the midst of the streets.
For all this his anger is not turned away, but his hand is
stretched out still [Isa. 5:25].**

"Therefore is the anger of the LORD kindled against his people." This is
a strange verse for many who want to talk about just the love of God.
The love of God is real, and you cannot keep Him from loving you; but
God hates sin, my friend. If you are going to love sin, still He will love
you, but you can expect His judgment. The anger of the Lord is kindled against *His* people—not against the neighbors.

"But his hand is stretched out still." If Israel had gone to the Lord
and trusted Him, He would have delivered them. The judgment of God
is in the Book of Isaiah but so is His grace. The government of God and
the grace of God—they are not in conflict. If you are going to continue
in sin, if you refuse the grace of God, then you *will* know what the
government of God is.

In the rest of this chapter we see an accumulation of the judgment
of God.

**And in that day they shall roar against them like the
roaring of the sea: and if one look unto the land, behold
darkness and sorrow, and the light is darkened in the
heavens thereof [Isa. 5:30].**

Take a good look at the land of Israel today. Many people who have
traveled to Israel come back and say, "It certainly is wonderful. We are
seeing the fulfillment of prophecy. The land is being reclaimed." They
go on and on about how prophecy is being fulfilled. I don't see it that
way at all. I see a people still in darkness. I see a people far from God. I
see a people who are not living in peace and who need God. They are
living in fear and are in great danger in that land today. My heart goes
out to them. This is the judgment of God.

Consider the following poem:

OUR PRAYERLESS SIN

We have not wept for thy grief,
   Israel, scattered, driven,
Shut up to darkened unbelief
   While we have heaven.

We have not prayed for thy peace,
   Jerusalem forsaken;
Thy root's increase, by God's great grace,
   We age-long have partaken.

How trod thy street our Saviour's feet;
   How fell His tears for thee;
How, loving Him, can we forget,
   Nor long thy joys to see.

Zion, thy God remembers thee
   Though we so hard have been;
Zion, thy God remembers thee,
   With blood-bought right to cleanse, may He
Remove our prayerless sin.
                  —Selected and revised

God is punishing His own pepole.

CHAPTER 6

THEME: The call and commission of Israel to the prophetic office

Chronologically, as well as logically, the Book of Isaiah begins with this chapter, which constitutes the crisis in the life of Isaiah and brings him into the prophetic office. Prior to this, we have no record of his life or relationship to God. His ministry began at the death of King Uzziah.

THE VISION OF THE LORD SEEN BY ISAIAH

In verses 1–4 are the time, place, person, glory, and holiness of the Lord in the vision seen by Isaiah. Now notice the time, the place, and the Person:

In the year that king Uzziah died I saw also the Lord sitting upon a throne, high and lifted up, and his train filled the temple [Isa. 6:1].

Isaiah opens this chapter on a very doleful note taking us to the funeral of Uzziah. Uzziah has been a good king. Now he is dead. It is the belief of many that he was the last great king of the southern kingdom of Judah and that after his death the glory of the Lord was no longer to be seen. I am not sure but what that is true. Uzziah brought the Philistines, the Arabians, and the Ammonites into subjection. He had ruled for fifty-two years, and the nation had been blessed materially during that period according to God's promise. As F. Delitzsch says, "The national glory of Israel died out too with King Uzziah and has never been recovered to this day." I heartily concur with that statement.

In the year that King Uzziah died, Isaiah is thinking, *Good King Uzziah is dead, and things are going to the bowwows now. Israel will be taken captive. Prosperity will cease. A depression will come, and famine will follow.* In that frame of mind Isaiah does what every person ought to do—he goes into the temple. He goes to the proper place, the place where he could meet with God. Psalm 29:9 says, ". . . in his temple doth everyone speak of his glory." In God's temple Isaiah makes the discovery that the true King of the nation is not dead.

"I saw also the Lord sitting upon a throne, high and lifted up, and his train filled the temple"—*God is on the throne.*

Isaiah has already told us not to put confidence in man, whose breath is in his nostrils. When man exhales, he doesn't know for sure that he ever will be able to inhale again. A man can have a heart attack and die, just like that. Don't put your confidence in man. Old King Uzziah is dead. Yes, it is true, and the throne looks pretty bleak right now but behind the earthly throne is the heavenly throne. Isaiah sees the Lord sitting upon a throne.

That is a vision that some of God's people need in this day. I see no reason for being pessimistic. This is the greatest day in the history of the world. I would rather live right now than in any other period of time. Somebody says, "Oh, look at the terrible condition of the world. Look at our nation and the deteriorating condition in our cities." Well, the Lord said it was going to be that way. He said that tares were going to be sown in among the wheat. And He was going to let them both grow together. My business today is sowing the seed of the Word of God. I know that it is going to bring forth a harvest. And it is heading up today—there is no question about that. We don't need to be disturbed. God will take care of the harvest. Our business is to sow the seed, that is, to get the Word of God out to needy hearts.

This is a great day in which to live. Do you know that the Word of God is going out to more people than it ever has before? Even my radio broadcast is reaching more people in a half hour than I was able to reach in all my years of preaching behind a pulpit. And the message is going around the world! I realize the world conditions are alarming. The tares are really growing, but we have a good stand of wheat also. The wheat is growing right along. It is thrilling to be sowing the Word of God in this day!

When Isaiah goes into the temple, he finds that the Lord is still on the throne. And some of us need to be reminded that God is still on the throne in our day. He still hears and answers prayers. He is still doing wonderful things. Isaiah also makes another discovery when he goes into the temple. He finds out that God is high and lifted up and that His train fills the temple. That is the second thing we need to discover about God. God is high and lifted up, and He will not compromise with sin.

Above it stood the seraphims: each one had six wings; with twain he covered his face, and with twain he covered his feet, and with twain he did fly [Isa. 6:2].

Seraphim are around the throne of God. This is one of the few mentions of these created intelligences in Scripture. Practically nothing is known concerning them. *Seraph* means "to burn." It is the word used in connection with the sin offerings and judgment. Apparently the seraphim are in contrast to the cherubim. The seraphim search out sin, and the cherubim protect the holiness of God. Never is the word *seraph* connected with the sweet incense or sweet savor offerings, those offerings which speak of the person of Christ. The seraph is active, and the cherub is passive. We will find both of them in the Books of Ezekial and Revelation as the "living creatures." The seraphim in Isaiah's vision are protecting the holiness of God. He is "high and lifted up."

God will not compromise with evil. I thank Him for that. He will not compromise with evil in your life, nor in my life, because evil and sin have brought all of the sorrows in this world. Sin is that which puts gray in the hair, creates the tottering step and the stooped shoulder. It is the thing that breaks up homes and lives, and fills the grave. I am glad that God does not compromise with it. God says that He hates sin and He intends to destroy it and remove it from this universe. Today our God is moving forth uncompromisingly, unhesitatingly, and undeviatingly against sin. He does not intend to accept the white flag of surrender from it. He intends to drive sin from His universe. That is what God says. He is high and lifted up. My friend, you and I are going to have to bow before Him. When Isaiah saw God on the throne, it brought him down upon his face. Oh, how desperately the church needs another vision of God, not just of His love, but of His holiness and righteousness! Because God is holy, He moves in judgment against sin—and He has never asked me to apologize for Him. So I won't. God is angry against sin, and He will punish those who engage in it. He *says* He will.

He also says that He is your Friend and will save you. But you have to come His way. You have to put your faith and trust in His Son, the Lord Jesus Christ. In John 14:6 Jesus said, ". . . I am the way, the truth, and the life: no man cometh unto the Father, but by me."

> **And one cried unto another, and said, Holy, holy, holy, is the LORD of hosts: the whole earth is full of his glory [Isa. 6:3].**

This pictures the holiness and glory of our God. He is high and lifted up; and, if we would see Him today in that position, we would be delivered from low living. It would also deliver some folk from this easy familiarity that they seem to have with Jesus. They talk about Him as if He were a buddy and as if they could speak to Him in any way they please. My friend, you cannot rush into the presence of God. He doesn't permit it. You come to the Father through Christ. This is the only way He can be approached. You can never come into the presence of the Father because of who you are. You come into His presence because you are *in Christ*. The Lord Jesus made that very clear when He said, "No man cometh unto the Father, but by me." If you are His child, you can come with boldness to the throne of grace, but you cannot come to Him on any other basis.

> **And the posts of the door moved at the voice of him that cried, and the house was filled with smoke [Isa. 6:4].**

"The voice of him that cried" is the voice of the seraphim as they proclaim God's holiness.

What effect is this going to have on Isaiah?

> **Then said I, Woe is me! for I am undone; because I am a man of unclean lips, and I dwell in the midst of a people**

**of unclean lips: for mine eyes have seen the King, the
LORD of hosts [Isa. 6:5].**

Isaiah was God's man before he had this experience, but it still had a
tremendous effect on him. The reaction of Isaiah to such a vision is
revolutionary. He sees himself as he really is in the presence of God—
undone. It reveals to him his condition. When he had seen God, he
could see himself. The problem with many of us today is that we don't
walk in the light of the Word of God. If we did, we would see ourselves. That is what John is talking about in the first chapter of his first
epistle: "But if we walk in the light, as he is in the light, we have
fellowship one with another, and the blood of Jesus Christ his Son
cleanseth [keeps on cleansing] us from all sin" (1 John 1:7). If we walk
in the light of His Word, we are going to see exactly what Isaiah saw—
that we are undone and men of unclean lips. You have never really
seen the Lord, my friend, if you feel that you are worthy, or merit something, or have some claim upon God.

Job had an experience similar to Isaiah's, and his reaction was "I
abhor myself." Job was a self-righteous man. He could maintain his
integrity in the presence of his friends who were attempting to tear
him to bits. They told him that he was a rotten sinner, but he looked
them straight in the eye and said, "As far as I know, I am a righteous
man." From his viewpoint he was right, and he won the match against
them. But he was not perfect. When Job came into the presence of God,
he no longer wanted to talk about maintaining his righteousness.
When Job really saw who he was, he said, "I have heard of thee by the
hearing of the ear: but now mine eye seeth thee. Wherefore I abhor
myself, and repent in dust and ashes" (Job 42:5-6). If you walk in the
light of the Word of God, you will see yourself, and you will know that
even as a child of God you need the blood of Jesus Christ to cleanse you
from all sin.

You will find that other men had the same reaction when they came
into the presence of God. John, on the Isle of Patmos, wrote, "And
when I saw him, I fell at his feet as dead . . ." (Rev. 1:17). When Daniel
saw the Lord, he said, "Therefore I was left alone, and saw this great

vision, and there remained no strength in me: for my comeliness was turned in me into corruption, and I retained no strength" (Dan. 10:8). That was also the experience of Saul of Tarsus, who became Paul the apostle. After Paul met the Lord, he no longer saw himself as a self-righteous Pharisee, but as a lost sinner in need of salvation. He then could say, "But what things were gain to me, those I counted loss for Christ" (Phil. 3:7). He saw his need of Jesus Christ.

> **Then flew one of the seraphims unto me, having a live coal in his hand, which he had taken with the tongs from off the altar [Isa. 6:6].**

This "live coal" has come from the burnt altar where sin had been dealt with. In the next chapter we will see the prediction of the birth of Christ, but it is not the incarnation of Christ that saves us, it is His death upon the cross. For this reason, Isaiah needs the live coal from off the burnt altar, which is symbolic of Christ's death. This living coal represents the cleansing blood of Christ that keeps on cleansing us from all sin.

> **And he laid it upon my mouth, and said, Lo, this hath touched thy lips; and thine iniquity is taken away, and thy sin purged [Isa. 6:7].**

Isaiah is a man of unclean lips, and the condition for cleansing is confession: "If we confess our sins, he is faithful and just to forgive us our sins, and to cleanse us from all unrighteousness" (1 John 1:9). I believe it would be more accurate to say that this glowing coal is symbolic of none other than the Lord Jesus Christ. He was the One high and lifted upon the throne, and He was the One lifted up on the cross. It is absolutely essential that He be lifted up, because He came down to this earth and became one of us that He might become ". . . the Lamb of God which taketh away the sin of the world" (John 1:29).

And so the lips of this man Isaiah are cleansed. I take it that this act of putting the coal on his lips was just an external manifestation of what happened in the inner man. It is what proceeds out of the heart of a man that goes through the lips; and, when the lips are cleansed, it means that the heart is cleansed also.

There was a man in the New Testament who also was "undone." His name was Paul, and he cried out, "O wretched man that I am! who shall deliver me from the body of this death?" (Rom. 7:24). When Paul said this, he was not a lost sinner but a saint of God, learning the lesson from God that he needed to walk in the Spirit because he could not live for God by himself. Living for God can only be accomplished by divine grace. Man's responsibility is to confess his sinfulness and his inability to please God. Therefore, we need to have the redemption of Christ applied to our lives again, and again, and again.

After Isaiah's lips are cleansed, something happens:

> **Also I heard the voices of the Lord, saying, Whom shall I send, and who will go for us? Then said I, Here am I; send me [Isa. 6:8].**

It is interesting that up to this time Isaiah had never heard the call of God.

I think many Christians have never felt like they were called to do anything for God because they have never been cleansed. They have not seen this great need as Christians. God is not going to use a dirty vessel, I can assure you of that. It is true that God does bless His Word even when it is given out by those who are playing around with sin, but in time God judges them severely. I don't dare mention any names, but I have known certain ministers who for awhile enjoyed the blessing of God. Then they got into sin, and it wasn't long until the judgment of God fell upon them.

Isaiah heard God's call: "Whom shall I send, and who will go for us?" I don't need to call attention to the fact that you have both the singular and the plural in this verse, and I believe it sets forth the Trinity. Isaiah's response was, "Here am I; send me." Isaiah heard God's call for the first time and responded to it, as a cleansed individual will do. There are too many people today who are asked to do something in the church who first of all ought to get cleansed and straightened out with the Lord. They need to have their lips touched with a living coal. They need to confess the sins in their lives, because their service will be sterile and frustrating until that takes place.

Now notice the commission to Isaiah:

And he said, Go, and tell this people, Hear ye indeed, but understand not; and see ye indeed, but perceive not [Isa. 6:9].

The message Isaiah is told to give is very, very strange. "This people" means, of course, the nation of Israel.

Make the heart of this people fat, and make their ears heavy, and shut their eyes; lest they see with their eyes, and hear with their ears, and understand with their heart, and convert, and be healed [Isa. 6:10].

At first glance it looks as if the prophet is being sent to those who are blind, deaf, and hardened people, but I think I can safely say that God never hardens hearts that would otherwise be soft. God simply brings the hardness to the surface; He does not make the heart hard. He does not make blind the eyes of those who want to see, but apart from His intervention they would never see. Nothing but the foolish blasphemy of men would say that God hardens or blinds.

Isaiah's job was to take a message of light to the people. Light merely reveals the blindness of the people. In darkness they do not know if they are blind or not. Matthew 13:14–15 records the words of our Lord: "And in them is fulfilled the prophecy of Esaias, which saith, By hearing ye shall hear, and shall not understand; and seeing ye shall see, and shall not perceive: For this people's heart is waxed gross, and their ears are dull of hearing, and their eyes they have closed; lest at any time they should see with their eyes, and hear with their ears, and should understand with their heart, and should be converted, and I should heal them."

Let me illustrate this. When I was a boy in Oklahoma, I used to have to milk a stubborn old cow. When it grew dark early in the evenings, I would have to take a lantern out to the barn with me. When I reached the corncrib two things would happen. The rats ran for cover—I could hear them taking off—and the little birds that were roosting up in the rafters would begin to twitter around and sing. The presence of light caused one to flee and the other to sing. Now, did the light make a rat a rat? No. He was a rat before the light got there. The light only revealed that he was a rat. When the Lord Jesus came into the world, He was the Light of the world. In His presence two things happened: He caused the birds to sing and the rats to run.

Let me illustrate this same thought with another story. Years ago there was a big explosion in a mine in West Virginia, and many men were blocked off in the mine because of the cave-ins. After several days a rescue party dug through to the trapped men. And one of the first things they managed to get through to them was a light. After the light came on, a fine young miner said, "Why doesn't someone turn on a light?" The other miners looked at him startled, suddenly realizing that he had been blinded by the explosion. But it took a light to reveal that he was blind.

God blinds nobody. He hardens no heart. When the light shines in, it reveals what an individual is, and that is what Isaiah means. That is exactly why the Lord Jesus Christ quoted this passage.

Paul wrote, "Now thanks be unto God, which always causeth us to triumph in Christ, and maketh manifest the savour of his knowledge by us in every place. For we are unto God a sweet savour of Christ, in them that are saved, and in them that perish: To the one we are the savour of death unto death; and to the other the savour of life unto life. And who is sufficient for these things?" (2 Cor. 2:14–16). I have often said, as I have given an invitation to receive Christ, "If you have rejected Christ—if you come into this church as a lost person and are leaving a lost person—I am no longer your friend, because you cannot now go into the presence of God and say that you never heard the gospel."

You see, the light of the gospel revealed that they were blind, and they rejected Jesus Christ. He didn't make them blind, but He only revealed their blindness.

"Now thanks be unto God, which always causeth us to triumph in

Christ"—we always triumph. There are those who like to boast of the number who are being saved, but I would much rather boast of the fact that thousands and even several millions of people are hearing the Word of God. My business is sowing the seed, the Word of God. It is the business of the Spirit of God to touch the hearts of those who hear.

CHAPTER 7

THEME: Prediction of the virgin birth of Immanuel and of Assyria's invasion of Judah

Verses 1 and 2 of this chapter speak of the civil war between Judah and Israel with Syria allied to Israel, resulting in a state of fear in Judah. Verses 3–9 tell us about the conduit of the upper pool where Isaiah and his son Shear-jashub meet Ahaz, king of Judah, with an encouraging word from the Lord. Verses 10–16 speak of the confirmation by the sign of the virgin birth to the house of David when Ahaz refuses to ask for a sign. Verses 17–25 tell of the coming invasion of the land of Judah by Assyria, which is predicted as a judgment.

And it came to pass in the days of Ahaz the son of Jotham, the son of Uzziah, king of Judah, that Rezin the king of Syria, and Pekah the son of Remaliah, king of Israel went up toward Jerusalem to war against it, but could not prevail against it [Isa. 7:1].

In 2 Kings 16:2 we read, "Twenty years old was Ahaz when he began to reign, and reigned sixteen years in Jerusalem, and did not that which was right in the sight of the LORD his God, like David his father." The prophecy of chapter 7 follows the call and commission of Isaiah in chapter 6, which took place at the death of Uzziah. Jotham, his son, succeeded him to the throne; and he reigned sixteen years. In 2 Kings 15:32–34 we are told, "In the second year of Pekah the son of Remaliah king of Israel began Jotham the son of Uzziah king of Judah to reign. Five and twenty years old was he when he began to reign, and he reigned sixteen years in Jerusalem. And his mother's name was Jerusha, the daughter of Zadok. And he did that which was right in the sight of the LORD: he did according to all that his father Uzziah had done." Jotham was a good king, as was his father Uzziah. Ahaz, Jotham's son, succeeds him, and he does that which is evil.

Ahaz will reign for sixteen years, and he will be a very bad king indeed. There will be a time of civil war during his reign. It will be a time of great distress in Israel. If you want to know just how bad things were, the record is in 2 Kings 16:3-4: "But he [Ahaz] walked in the way of the kings of Israel, yea, and made his son to pass through the fire, according to the abominations of the heathen, whom the LORD cast out from before the children of Israel. And he sacrificed and burnt incense in the high places, and on the hills, and under every green tree." Ahaz is a bad egg, I can assure you of that, and he is frightened because Israel in the north teamed up with Syria, and they are coming against him. Although they do not prevail at first, Ahaz has every reason to believe that they finally will prevail.

> **And it was told the house of David, saying, Syria is confederate with Ephraim. And his heart was moved, and the heart of his people as the trees of the wood are moved with the wind [Isa. 7:2].**

Ahaz cannot expect the blessing of God upon him or the nation. As a result, the alliance of Rezin, king of Syria, with Pekah, king of Israel, terrifies him and his people. Previously both Syria and Israel had attempted to take Judah. Alone they could not prevail, but together Ahaz is confident that they will be able to take Jerusalem. In spite of the fact that Ahaz is a godless king, God is not yet ready to let the people of Judah go into captivity. As we already know from history, Judah is not going to go into captivity in the north, but many years later they will be taken captive to Babylon.

> **Then said the LORD unto Isaiah, Go forth now to meet Ahaz, thou, and Shear-jashub thy son, at the end of the conduit of the upper pool in the highway of the fuller's field [Isa. 7:3].**

Because God is not ready to deliver the kingdom of Judah into captivity, He wants to encourage the king so he will not make an unwise and frantic alliance with Egypt. So God tells Isaiah to meet with Ahaz.

There are several things we need to look at in this verse. First of all, Isaiah is to meet Ahaz "at the end of the conduit of the upper pool." The place where he is to meet the king is suggestive. It is from this conduit that the life-giving waters pour for thirsty Jerusalem. It is here that the people can quench their thirst. You can't get much satisfaction from a pipe filled with water—you must have a spigot on it somewhere. You must go to the place where the water comes out of the pipe.

Now this is symbolic of the fact that you are not going to get any blessing out of that house of David, but way down at the end of his line One is coming as the "water of life." That One was the Lord Jesus Christ. He came in the line of David to bring the water of life.

Isaiah is to meet the king at the upper "pool." The word for "pool" is *berekah* from the root word meaning "blessing." I can assure you that in that land a pool of water is a blessing. This same word used in Psalm 84:6, ". . . the rain also filleth the pools [*berakah*]," everywhere else is rendered "blessing." This is a very interesting thing.

Notice also that it is "the upper pool." *Upper* is the word used over thirty times for the Most High. You may recall that it was said of the one who came out to minister to Abraham that he was the priest of the Most High God (see Gen. 14:18). Now the blessing of the Most High God was given "at the end of the conduit" when Jesus came into the world.

"In the highway of the fuller's field." The highway is a path which is elevated above the surrounding land to keep the traveler's feet clean. The spiritual application of the word *highway* is made clear in Proverbs 16:17: "The highway of the upright is to depart from evil. . . ." This highway is the way of holiness. Isaiah will use this same figure in Isaiah 35:8: "And an highway shall be there, and a way, and it shall be called The way of holiness." This very interesting symbolism refers to the One who is the way, the truth, and the life. The psalmist wrote in Pslams 84:5: "Blessed is the man whose strength is in thee; in whose heart are the ways of them." That is, blessed is the one who has the One who is the way, the truth, and the life.

Notice also that the meeting was to take place in the "fuller's field." The fuller's field was the place where folk went to wash their clothes. It was the laundry of that day. Applying this to our own lives, if we want to get our lives cleansed, we must come to the Lord Jesus Christ. He said, ". . . ye are clean through the word which I have spoken unto you" (John 15:3).

So you see, it is no accident that Isaiah is sent to this very interesting place for his meeting with Ahaz. It has a wonderful spiritual meaning for us.

Isaiah is told to take his son Shear-jashub with him. That is quite a name for a boy, but it is nothing compared to the second son whom we shall meet in chapter 8. *Shear-jashub* means "a remnant shall return." The interesting thing is that God has always had a remnant that was true to Him.

> **And say unto him, Take heed, and be quiet; fear not, neither be fainthearted for the two tails of these smoking firebrands, for the fierce anger of Rezin with Syria, and of the son of Remaliah.**
>
> **Because Syria, Ephraim, and the son of Remaliah, have taken evil counsel against thee, saying,**
>
> **Let us go up against Judah, and vex it, and let us make a breach therein for us, and set a king in the midst of it, even the son of Tabeal:**
>
> **Thus saith the Lord God, It shall not stand, neither shall it come to pass.**
>
> **For the head of Syria is Damascus, and the head of Damascus is Rezin; and within threescore and five years shall Ephraim be broken, that it be not a people.**
>
> **And the head of Ephraim is Samaria, and the head of Samaria is Remaliah's son. If ye will not believe, surely ye shall not be established [Isa. 7:4-9].**

The tenor of the message is to let Ahaz know that he need not fear the alliance of his two enemies in the north. God has determined that their venture will be a failure. The problem is, how will Ahaz know it? To begin with, he is a skeptic, a doubter, and an unbeliever. How will he be convinced that what Isaiah is saying is true?

God has never asked anyone to believe anything that does not rest upon a foundation. Faith does not mean to move blindly into some area and say, "Oh, I am trusting God." That is very foolish. God never asks us to do that. For example, in our salvation we do not bring a little lamb to offer as a sacrifice; our faith rests upon the historical facts of the death, the burial and the resurrection of the Son of God. God never asks us to take a leap in the dark. He asks us to believe and trust something which rests upon a firm foundation, and it is the *only* foundation, "For other foundation can no man lay than that is laid, which is Jesus Christ" (1 Cor. 3:11). If any person is an honest unbeliever and sincerely wants to know God, he will come to a saving faith. Folk with whom I have dealt who say that they cannot believe are not being honest. For example, a young fellow in San Francisco told me, "Oh, I want to believe; I am searching for the truth." There he was, living with a girl in an adulterous relationship and saying that he was searching for the truth! The fact of the matter is that no man's eyes are blindfolded unless he himself choses to be blindfolded. If a person really wants to know God and will give up his sin and turn to Christ, God will make Himself real to him. In our day the problem is that a great many folk do not really mean business with God.

That is the problem with King Ahaz—he doesn't mean business with God. Listen to him—

Moreover the LORD spake again unto Ahaz, saying,

Ask thee a sign of the LORD thy God; ask it either in the depth, or in the height above [Isa. 7:10-11].

God knows that Ahaz does not have faith, and He is willing to give the king faith; but Ahaz is nothing but a pious fraud—and there are a lot of those around today. Listen to his false piety:

But Ahaz said, I will not ask, neither will I tempt the LORD [Isa. 7:12].

Isn't that sweet of him? He sounds so nice, but he is one of the biggest
hypocrites you will find in Scripture. This sort of thing is sickening,
and I believe God feels that way about it.

**And he said, Hear ye now, O house of David; Is it a small
thing for you to weary men, but will ye weary my God
also? [Isa. 7:13].**

I hope you won't mind my telling a little story. One day, in a Sunday
school class for junior boys and girls, the teacher was telling the story
about the Good Samaritan. As she related the parable, she was paint-
ing a vivid picture. She told how the man fell among thieves, how he
was beaten up, and blood was gushing out from the wounds in his
body. She told about the priest, and the Pharisee, and finally she came
to the Good Samaritan. She wanted to clinch her presentation by making an application to the lives of the children. She first asked a little
girl, "What would you have done?" She said, "Oh, I would have stayed
and nursed him for a few days." The next little boy didn't want to be
outdone, so he said, "And I would have brought him a box of candy."
The teacher went around the class with her question, and finally came
to a little girl who had a very distressed look on her face. The teacher
said to her, "What would you have done?" She said, "I think I would
have *thrown up!*" Believe me, the teacher had painted a gory picture,
and that little girl was being honest.

I think God feels that way about our piousness. My friend, don't
think you are being pious when you say, "Oh, I won't test God." God
says, "Test Me. Try Me, and see if I am not good." I actually feel fa-
tigued when I talk to some folk who say that they are just going to step
out on "faith." Oh, my friend, wait until God puts a rock underneath
you. Wait until God gives you definite leading before you make a fool
of yourself and bring criticism upon the cause of Christ.

God says to this unbelieving king, "I'm not asking you to believe
My message just because Isaiah said it. I want to put a foundation under it. I want to give you a supernatural sign so you will know that the
message is from Me." But Ahaz refuses to ask for a sign. So God is
going to give a sign—not to Ahaz—but to the whole house of David.

Therefore the Lord himself shall give you a sign; Behold, a virgin shall conceive, and bear a son, and shall call his name Immanuel [Isa. 7:14].

God puts a foundation under His prophecy; and, if you want to know whether or not the virgin birth is true, you can find out if you read the four Gospels. For example, in Matthew we read, "Now the birth of Jesus Christ was on this wise: When as his mother Mary was espoused to Joseph, before they came together, she was found with child of the Holy Ghost. Then Joseph her husband, being a just man, and not willing to make her a public example, was minded to put her away privily. But while he thought on these things, behold, the angel of the Lord appeared unto him in a dream, saying, Joseph, thou son of David, fear not to take unto thee Mary thy wife: for that which is conceived in her is of the Holy Ghost. And she shall bring forth a son, and thou shalt call his name JESUS: for he shall save his people from their sins. Now all this was done, that it might be fulfilled which was spoken of the Lord by the prophet, saying, Behold, a virgin shall be with child, and shall bring forth a son, and they shall call his name Emmanuel, which being interpreted is, God with us" (Matt. 1:18–23).

Isaiah 7:14 has become one of the most controversial verses in Scripture because of the prophecy concerning the virgin birth. Unbelievers have quite naturally discounted it and have sought desperately, but in vain, for a loophole to reject the virgin birth. The battle has been waged about the meaning of Hebrew word *almah*, which is translated "virgin."

The fact that the angel quotes this prophecy in Isaiah 7:14 to Joseph as an explanation for Mary's being with child before her marriage to him is satisfactory evidence that the prophecy referred to an unmarried woman who had a son without physical contact with any man. The word used by Matthew (see Matt. 1:23) is the Greek word *parthenos*, which definitely means "virgin." The same Greek word was used for the Parthenon, the Greek temple to the goddess Athena, which the Greeks characterized as being a virgin.

When the Revised Standard Version of the Bible was first published, the Hebrew word *almah* was translated "young woman," with "virgin" in the footnotes—of course, it should have been reversed. Their argument was that *almah* meant only a young woman. While it is true that there are places in the Scriptures where it is translated "young woman," it is evident that it means "virgin."

For example, when Abraham's servant went to Haran in search of a bride for Isaac and he prayed that God would direct him to the right girl, this is how Rebekah was described: "And the damsel was very fair to look upon, a virgin, neither had any man known her . . ." (Gen. 24:16). The word *damsel* is the Hebrew word *naarah*, meaning "young woman," but that she was a virgin was made clear also. Then when the servant was rehearsing this experience of praying for God's guidance, he said, "Behold, I stand by the well of water; and it shall come to pass, that when the virgin cometh forth to draw water . . ." (Gen. 24:43), the Hebrew word *almah* is translated "virgin." I don't think that anyone could misunderstand what is being said here. When the word *almah* was used, it referred to a virgin young woman, that is, one who had had no sexual relationship with a man.

When the liberal theologian says that the Bible does not teach the virgin birth of Jesus, I feel like asking him if his papa had talked to him when he was a boy about the birds and the bees. He can deny that he believes in the virgin birth of Jesus, but he cannot deny that Isaiah and Matthew are talking about the virgin birth of Jesus.

Notice again Isaiah's prophecy: "Behold, a virgin shall conceive, and bear a son, and shall call his name Immanuel." Isaiah said that His name would be Immanuel, but you cannot find any place in the Gospels where He is called by that name. *Immanuel* means "God with us." They called Him "Jesus" because He would save His people from their sins. But, friend, He cannot save the people from their sins unless He is Immanuel, "God with us." Everytime you call Him Jesus, you are saying, "God with us." He is God. He is God with us and God for us. He is our Savior, born of a virgin. Have you put your trust in Him?

When Isaiah gave this prophecy in 7:14, someone probably came to him and said, "When will this take place?" I have a notion that Isaiah looked down through the centuries and said, "It will be a long time." Then how would the people of his generation know the prediction was

true? The virgin birth of Christ would come to pass, just as Isaiah said
it would, because God had spoken through Isaiah on many other
things that were fulfilled during the days in which he spoke them.
One of them was his prophecy about Hezekiah and the Assyrians,
which we shall see in the historic section of Isaiah. The Assyrians
once gathered outside the walls of Jerusalem, and they were 150,000
strong. Things looked bad for Jerusalem. It looked as if the city would
fall. So Hezekiah went into the temple, got down on his knees, and fell
on his face before God. He cried out for deliverance, and God sent
Isaiah to him with a message. Isaiah told Hezekiah that he didn't have
to worry. The Assyrians would not come into the city, nor would they
take it. In fact, Isaiah told the king that not even one arrow would be
shot into Jerusalem. There were 150,000 soldiers outside the walls of
Jerusalem and each soldier had a quiver full of arrows on his back and
a bow in his hand. You would think that out of that many soldiers there
would be one that was trigger-happy, one who would shoot an arrow
over the wall just to see if anyone would yell. If just one soldier had
shot one arrow over the wall into the city, Isaiah would have rightly
been declared a false prophet. But no arrows were shot; the city was
spared. What Isaiah had told Hezekiah came true. And the New Testament bears witness to the fact that the virgin birth of the Lord Jesus
came to pass exactly as Isaiah had predicted.

> **Butter and honey shall he eat, that he may know to**
> **refuse the evil, and choose the good [Isa. 7:15].**

Jesus was reared as a poor peasant in Palestine. This food was the
simple diet of the poor.

> **For before the child shall know to refuse the evil, and**
> **choose the good, the land that thou abhorrest shall be**
> **forsaken of both her kings [Isa. 7:16].**

This verse would be fulfilled by the time the Messiah came. This
seemed unlikely in Ahaz' day.

CHAPTER 8

THEME: The birth of the prophet's second son as a sign; prediction of Assyria's invasion of Immanuel's land

Chapters 7—12 constitute a series of prophecies given during the reign of Ahaz. Some have attempted to identify the virgin's Son of chapter 7 with the prophet's son in chapter 8. The names preclude that possibility, and the additional information in chapter 9 makes it an impossibility for the two to be identical. The prophet's son is a sign (see v. 18).

This chapter is rather significant as it contains the prediction of the invasion of Immanuel's land by the king of Assyria. God had kept the flood tide of foreign invasions walled off from His people for over five hundred years. Now He opens the floodgates and permits an enemy to cover the land like a flood. The people are looking to a confederacy rather than looking to God for help.

This chapter concludes with a warning against spiritualism as the last resort of people who have rejected God's counsel and turned in desperation to the satanic world. The end will be trouble, darkness, and anguish.

THE BIRTH OF THE PROPHET'S
SECOND SON AS A SIGN

Moreover the Lord said unto me, Take thee a great roll, and write in it with a man's pen concerning Maher-shalal-hash-baz [Isa. 8:1].

If you thought Shear-jashub was a strange name for a boy, try this one on for size! Maher-shalal-hash-baz is a remarkable name for a boy in any language. How would you like to carry this cognomen through life? That's what Isaiah's son had to do. I don't know what his nickname was. They may have shortened his name to Maher, or Hash, or even Baz. There is a reason, however, why God wants Isaiah to give his sons these unusual names. The reason is found in verse 18 which says, "Behold, I and the children whom the LORD hath given me are for signs and for wonders in Israel from the LORD of hosts, which dwelleth in mount Zion." Both sons are signs, and their names carry a message.

Maher-shalal-hash-baz means "hasten booty, speed prey." This simply means that God is against those who are against His people. Paul put it like this: ". . . If God be for us, who can be against us?" (Rom. 8:31).

This boy's name is also a message for Ahaz, the man on the throne. He is a godless man, and God is trying to reach him. He tells Isaiah to get a great tablet, and write on it with a "man's pen"—or, the stylus of a frail, mortal man. He is then to hang it up in a prominent place like a billboard so that everyone can read it. God wants this boy's name written down so that the most humble person in the kingdom will see it, read it, and understand it. God is trying to reach Ahaz, first through Isaiah's first son, Shear-jashub ("a remnant shall return") and then through Maher-shalal-hash-baz ("hasten booty, speed prey"). This second son's name is to assure Ahaz that God will take care of the enemies of His people.

And I took unto me faithful witnesses to record, Uriah the priest, and Zechariah the son of Jeberechiah [Isa. 8:2].

Uriah means "Jehovah is my light." *Zechariah* means "Jehovah remembers." *Jeberechiah* means "Jehovah will bless." This is an interesting combination, is it not? Thus, the one witness says by his name, "Jehovah is my light," and the other says, "Jehovah's purpose is to bless." The offspring of these is the grace of God—that is, He will never forget His people.

In all of Isaiah's actions there is a message for the people. He is acting out and writing out his message so that the people will understand it. The Book of Isaiah is a picture parable. Our Lord used this method also. The reason is that people will look at a picture. It is

somewhat like television. It is amazing how many of us will sit in front
of the television screen and watch things from that idiot box which
under different circumstances we wouldn't waste our time on. Because God knows the inclination of mankind, He tries to get a message
across to these people by using a picture.

> **And I went unto the prophetess; and she conceived, and
> bare a son. Then said the LORD to me, Call his name
> Maher-shalal-hash-baz [Isa. 8:3].**

"The prophetess" in this verse is Isaiah's wife, Mrs. Isaiah. She con-
ceives and bears a son, and the child's name is given to him before he
is born.

> **For before the child shall have knowledge to cry, My
> father, and my mother, the riches of Damascus and the
> spoil of Samaria shall be taken away before the king of
> Assyria [Isa. 8:4].**

Before this child is able to say "Mommy" and "Daddy," the Assyrians
will invade Syria and Samaria. The enemy in the north that is planning to come against Judah is going to be taken away into captivity. It
will not be due to the brilliant military ability of Ahaz to work out a
strategy that will bring victory. The victory will be due to the sovereign grace of God—God is making this perfectly clear.

> **The LORD spake also unto me again, saying,**

> **Forasmuch as this people refuseth the waters of Shiloah
> that go softly, and rejoice in Rezin and Remaliah's son;**

> **Now therefore, behold, the Lord bringeth up upon them
> the waters of the river, strong and many, even the king of
> Assyria, and all his glory: and he shall come up over all
> his channels, and go over all his banks [Isa. 8:5–7].**

This is another remarkable passage of Scripture. The people "refuseth
the waters of Shiloah," which means "sent." They refuse the peace

God offered them, a peace here typified by this gentle, rippling brook. In contrast, we see in verse 7 "the waters of the river, strong and many." This is evidently the Euphrates River where Assyria was located. These waters came down like a flood. In other words, the flood waters of the Euphrates represent the judgment of God and are contrasted with the gentle waters of Shiloah. God is giving a message to His people through these two rivers. As Shakespeare put it in his play *As You Like It*, there are "tongues in trees, books in the running brooks, sermons in stones, and good in everything."

Shiloah is a softly flowing little spring. It doesn't amount to much today, but it did in Isaiah's day. It flows between Mount Zion and Mount Moriah. There is a message in that little stream, a message that you will hear if you have a blood-tipped ear. It is a message sweeter than the rippling music of the stream itself. It is the story of grace, of Mount Zion, which stands in contrast to Mount Sinai, which is symbolic of the Mosaic Law. Moriah is where Abraham offered his son, where David bought the threshingfloor of Araunah, and where Solomon put up the temple. And down at the end of that great shaft of rocks is Golgotha, where Christ was crucified. This speaks of grace. Moriah is where God provided Himself a Lamb. He spared Abraham's son, but He did not spare His own Son.

So here God is speaking grace to this man, Ahaz. He is saying to him, "I'll spare you, if only you will turn to Me."

And he shall pass through Judah; he shall overflow and go over, he shall reach even to the neck; and the stretching out of his wings shall fill the breadth of thy land, O Immanuel [Isa. 8:8].

God will permit Assyrians to overflow the land of Judah, but He will never permit them to take Jerusalem.

PRONOUNCEMENT AGAINST A CONFEDERACY AS A SUBSTITUTE FOR GOD

Associate yourselves, O ye people, and ye shall be broken in pieces; and give ear, all ye of far countries: gird

**yourselves, and ye shall be broken in pieces; gird your-
selves, and ye shall be broken in pieces [Isa. 8:9].**

This is a warning against nations who form an alliance against God's
land. Beginning with Isaiah 13, we are going to have a series of messages to the nations that were contiguous to Israel, or at least had dealings with them in that day, and we will find the judgment of God will
come upon them. That section which goes all the way from Isaiah 13
to Isaiah 35 is a most remarkable section in God's Word. Most of it is
fulfilled prophecy. God says that the nations will never deter His purpose here on earth. It is interesting that the nations of the world no
longer seek wisdom or counsel from God. God does have a purpose,
and his purpose *will* prevail. If a nation goes in the other direction,
judgment will come upon it.

**Take counsel together, and it shall come to nought;
speak the word, and it shall not stand: for God is with
us.**

**For the Lord spake thus to me with a strong hand, and
instructed me that I should not walk in the way of this
people, saying,**

**Say ye not, A confederacy, to all them to whom this peo-
ple shall say, A confederacy; neither fear ye their fear,
nor be afraid [Isa. 8:10–12].**

Judah is not to be alarmed by the confederacy of Syria and Samaria.
Fear had caused those in the north to unite, and God urges His people,
"neither fear ye their fear." In other words, they are not to turn to an
ally among the nations, which probably would have been Egypt. Later
on they will ally themselves with Egypt, which brings great tragedy to
the land.

**Sanctify the Lord of hosts himself; and let him be your
fear, and let him be your dread.**

And he shall be for a sanctuary; but for a stone of stumbling and for a rock of offence to both the houses of Israel, for a gin and for a snare to the inhabitants of
Jerusalem [Isa. 8:13-14].

They are to fear God above and look to Him. He will be either their
salvation or a stone of stumbling. Cromwell was once asked why he
was such a brave man. He had the reputation of being one of the brav-
est men who ever lived. He said, "I have learned that when you fear
God, you have no man to fear." Paul said in 1 Cor. 1:23, "But we preach
Christ crucified, unto the Jews a stumblingblock, and unto the Greeks
foolishness." The Lord Jesus said that either you will fall on this
stone—and He is that stone—fall on Him for salvation, rest upon Him
who is the only foundation, and you will be saved; or He, the stone,
will fall on you, judge you, and it will grind you to powder (see Matt.
21:44). You have two options: you can either accept Him or reject Him.

"Sanctify the LORD of hosts himself" is a strange injunction. Peter
used this: "But sanctify the Lord God in your hearts: and be ready
always to give an answer to every man that asketh you a reason of the
hope that is in you with meekness and fear" (1 Pet. 3:15). This is what
God's people need to do. Today there is this light thinking about God,
a lack of reverence for Him and for His Word. There are those who
sometimes ridicule things that are sacred, make light of things that
should not be made light of. You and I need to sanctify the Lord God in
our hearts, because there are multitudes of people today who are not
convinced that ". . . the LORD is in his holy temple: let all the earth keep
silence before him" (Hab. 2:20). If they believed, my friend, that He is
in your church on Sunday morning, they would not be at the beach, at
some picnic area, or out mowing the back lawn. They would be with
you in church. You and I haven't convinced them, have we?

PRONOUNCEMENT AGAINST SPIRITUALISM AS
A SUBSTITUTE FOR THE WORD OF GOD

And when they shall say unto you, Seek unto them that
have familiar spirits, and unto wizards that peep, and

that mutter: should not a people seek unto their God? for the living to the dead? [Isa. 8:19].

We are seeing a resurgence of spiritualism today. More than fifteen years ago I wrote, "God forbids His people to dabble in this satanic system. When a people turn from God, they generally go after the occult and abnormal" (see Lev. 20:27; Deut. 18:9–12).

There is a great turning today to the occult, to the spirit world, and to demonology. There are churches of Satan in Southern California and in the San Francisco Bay area. The members worship the Devil; many are worshiping Satan today. Even Christians are dabbling in the occult. Many of them talk about casting out demons. My friend, I am not in that business. I preach the gospel of the grace of God and the Word of God. That will take care of all the demons. I say that we need to let the occult alone because it is dangerous, and it is growing by leaps and bounds. Some people don't believe there is any reality in it, but it is real, just as Satan is real. God warns us against it. Let us heed that warning.

And they shall pass through it, hardly bestead and hungry: and it shall come to pass, that when they shall be hungry, they shall fret themselves, and curse their king and their God, and look upward.

And they shall look unto the earth; and behold trouble and darkness, dimness of anguish; and they shall be driven to darkness [Isa. 8:21–22].

These final verses reveal the final issue of pursuing a life of disobedience which will lead you into spiritualism. The result is dimness, darkness, and despair. Disobedience will take you there every time.

CHAPTER 9

THEME: Prophecy of the Child coming to David's throne and the dark days attending His first coming and preceding His second coming

This chapter is one with which Christians are generally familiar because of the prophecy concerning the coming Child, who is Christ. Handel's use of this chapter in *The Messiah* has added to the familiarity of the church with this particular passage. I am always thrilled when I listen to a presentation of Handel's work, especially when they sing, "And his name shall be called Wonderful, Counsellor, The mighty God, The everlasting Father, The Prince of Peace."

The material presented in Isaiah 7—12 contains prophecies that Isaiah made during the reign of Ahaz. Ahaz was the one bad king that reigned during the period in which Isaiah prophesied. Isaiah began to prophesy at the death of Uzziah, who reigned for fifty-two years and was a good king. The next king was Jotham, Uzziah's son, who was also a good king. The next king was Ahaz, the grandson of Uzziah and the son of Jotham, who was a bad king and a phony besides. It was during the reign of Ahaz that Isaiah made these prophecies concerning the Messiah. It was a dark period in the history of the nation.

THE HOPE OF ISRAEL

In verses 1–7 we find that the hope of Israel is in the divine Child in both His first and second comings.

> **Nevertheless the dimness shall not be such as was in her vexation, when at the first he lightly afflicted the land of Zebulun and the land of Naphtali, and afterward did more grievously afflict her by the way of the sea, beyond Jordan, in Galilee of the nations [Isa. 9:1].**

The translation of this verse is not established. Actually, contrary meanings are suggested. This poses no problem to the reverent mind but reveals a divine purpose in permitting both to be possible.

"And afterward did more grievously afflict her by the way of the sea, beyond Jordan, in Galilee of the nations." Others have translated it: "But in the latter time hath he made it glorious, by the way of the sea, beyond the Jordan, Galilee of the nations." It is difficult to see how both translations, "more grievously afflict" and "made it glorious," can be sustained, but I believe it is enigmatic for a reason. The first translation would refer to the near fulfillment when God did afflict the northeastern portion of the land comparatively lightly in the invasions of the Syrians and later brought heavier suffering upon them in the carrying away of the people into captivity by the Assyrians (see 2 Kings 15:29).

But the other translation, "hath he made it glorious," refers to the far fulfillment in the first coming of Christ. He *did* "make glorious" that area. Galilee was the despised area because it was a place where Gentiles had congregated. The Lord Jesus passed by Jerusalem, the snobbish religious center of the day. Jesus was neither born nor reared in Jerusalem. Nazareth was His hometown; and, when Nazareth rejected Him, He went down to Capernaum, which is on the Sea of Galilee in the despised periphery of the kingdom. Zebulun and Naphtali were located in the north, with Naphtali along the west bank of the Sea of Galilee and Zebulun adjoining Naphtali on the west. Nazareth was in Zebulun, and Capernaum (Jesus' headquarters) was in Naphtali. As far as I can tell, the Lord Jesus never changed His headquarters from Capernaum. In fact, that explains why He pronounced such a severe judgment upon Capernaum—it had access to light as no other place had.

Matthew 4:12–16 tells us, "Now when Jesus had heard that John was cast into prison, he departed into Galilee; And leaving Nazareth, he came and dwelt in Capernaum, which is upon the sea coast, in the borders of Zabulon and Nephthalim: That it might be fulfilled which was spoken by Esaias the prophet, saying, The land of Zabulon, and the land of Nephthalim, by the way of the sea, beyond Jordan, Galilee of the Gentiles; The people which sat in darkness saw great light; and to them which sat in the region and shadow of death light is sprung up." You will note that Matthew omitted the questionable clause. Otherwise, we would have the Holy Spirit's own interpretation of the passage. I believe that the double meaning is intended by the Holy Spirit. Both are surely true.

> **The people that walked in darkness have seen a great light: they that dwell in the land of the shadow of death, upon them hath the light shined [Isa. 9:2].**

Regardless of the way verse 1 is translated or interpreted, it is obvious that the people in despised Galilee were in the darkness of paganism and religious tradition. That is one place where the Old Testament and paganism from the outside mingled and mixed. When the Lord Jesus began His ministry in that area, the people did see a great light. They saw the Lord Jesus Christ, the Light of the world. "Then spake Jesus again unto them, saying, I am the light of the world: he that followeth me shall not walk in darkness, but shall have the light of life" (John 8:12). This was fulfilled at the first coming of Christ. I think it is safe to say that the first two verses refer to our Lord's first coming.

But to what period do the following verses refer? It is the belief of certain outstanding Bible expositors, among whom are Dr. F. C. Jennings and Dr. H. A. Ironside, that there is a hiatus, an interval, between verses 2 and 3, so that while the first two verses refer to Christ's first coming, verse 3 refers to His second coming, as we shall see.

> **Thou hast multiplied the nation, and not increased the joy: they joy before thee according to the joy in harvest, and as men rejoice when they divide the spoil [Isa. 9:3].**

The nation had been greatly multiplied and the people were more religious, but the joy was gone. They had a lot of religion, but they never had Christ. It was a period of great manifestation but no real joy.

The hiatus between verses 2 and 3 has already been two thousand years long. Why didn't Isaiah give any prophecy about this period? Because during this interval God is calling out the church which was unknown to Isaiah. In Romans 16:25–26 Paul says, "Now to him that is of power to stablish you according to my gospel, and the preaching of Jesus Christ, according to the revelation of the mystery, which was kept secret since the world began, But now is made manifest, and by the scriptures of the prophets, according to the commandment of the everlasting God, made known to all nations for the obedience of faith." Paul makes it very clear that the prophets passed over that which they did not see, as Isaiah does in the chapter before us. In Isaiah 63 we will come to a place where with just a comma Isaiah passes over a period of time that is already two thousand years long. The people in Isaiah's day had no revelation concerning the church, but today the church has been revealed and the interval is filled in. This makes it clear that the rest of this chapter refers to the nation Israel, and the nation that was "multiplied" was the nation over which Ahaz was king. Notice that Paul says it was "made known to *all* nations for the obedience of faith." So, you see, the revelation of the church was for a different congregation. Isaiah was speaking only to one nation, his own nation of Israel.

For thou hast broken the yoke of his burden, and the staff of his shoulder, the rod of his oppressor, as in the day of Midian [Isa. 9:4].

When will the burden be broken? It will be broken when Christ comes again. Why is it that Israel today cannot enjoy peace? Why are they plagued along every border? They are having all this trouble because they rejected the only One who can bring peace, their own Messiah, the Lord Jesus Christ. The power of the oppressor will not be broken until the Lord comes the second time.

For every battle of the warrior is with confused noise, and garments rolled in blood; but this shall be with burning and fuel of fire [Isa. 9:5].

What a sad thing it was when those fine young Jewish athletes were killed during the Olympic Games in Munich a few years ago. They were murdered by terrorists; and, when their bodies were sent back to

Israel, their loved ones and the whole nation mourned. What is in back of all this? Israel has a Messiah whom they have rejected. He is the Prince of Peace, and He is the only One who can bring peace to this troubled and persecuted people.

While these verses complete the thought of verse 3, they also look beyond the immediate time of the Great Tribulation Period which is coming in the future.

Now we see the prediction of their Messiah's coming:

> **For unto us a child is born, unto us a son is given: and the government shall be upon his shoulder: and his name shall be called Wonderful, Counsellor, The mighty God, The everlasting Father, The Prince of Peace.**
>
> **Of the increase of his government and peace there shall be no end, upon the throne of David, and upon his kingdom, to order it, and to establish it with judgment and with justice from henceforth even for ever. The zeal of the LORD of hosts will perform this [Isa. 9:6–7].**

How will this come about? "The zeal of the LORD of hosts will perform this." Is this a reference to the first coming of Christ? Most Christians seem to think it is, because they quote it at Christmas time. However, I feel sure that it refers to the second coming of Christ when he will be "born" to the nation of Israel. This is a complete prophecy of the Lord Jesus Christ at His second coming, as Isaiah 53 is of His first coming. These verses continue the thought which we picked up in verse 3, and they look forward to the second coming of Christ.

The question arises of how "a child is born" at His second coming. First of all, let me clearly state that He was not born "unto us," the nation Israel, at His first coming. They didn't receive Him. "He came unto his own, and his own received him not" (John 1:11). Although He was born at Bethlehem the first time, He was not received by the nation—only a few shepherds welcomed Him. The wise men who came to worship Him were Gentiles from a foreign land. If you read verse 6 carefully, you will see that it was not fulfilled at His first coming, nor were verses 3, 5, and 7.

To say that Christ will be born to the nation Israel might be better stated. Actually, Israel will be born as a nation "at once," which is made perfectly clear in the final chapter of Isaiah: "Before she travailed, she brought forth; before her pain came, she was delivered of a man child. Who hath heard such a thing? who hath seen such things? Shall the earth be made to bring forth in one day? or shall a nation be born at once? for as soon as Zion travailed [that is the Great Tribulation], she brought forth her children" (Isa. 66:7–8).

Israel is to be "delivered of a man child" in the future, not by His birth, but by Israel's birth. This will be the new birth of the nation Israel when Christ comes again. Israel will be born at the second coming of Christ.

I see no objection to calling attention to the fact that the child is *born*—that is, His humanity. The son is *given*, which will be true at His second coming. In other words, it will be the same Jesus who was here nearly two thousand years go.

"The government shall be upon his shoulder." The shoulder speaks of strength. The government of this world will be placed on His strong shoulders at His second coming; it was not at His first coming.

Notice the names that are given to our Lord:

"Wonderful"—this is not an adjective; this is His name. In Judges 13:18 we see the preincarnate Christ appearing as the Captain of the hosts of the Lord: "And the angel of the LORD said unto him, Why askest thou thus after my name, seeing it is secret?" "Secret" in this verse is the same word as is translated "Wonderful." In Matthew 11:27 the Lord Jesus said, ". . . no man knoweth the Son, but the Father. . . ." The people did not know it, but He was Wonderful, and people still don't know it today. There are Christians who have trusted Him as Savior but really don't know how wonderful He is.

He is going to put down rebellion when He comes to earth the second time, and He is going to reign on earth. His name is "Wonderful!"

"Counsellor"—He never sought the counsel of man, and He never asked for the advice of man. "For who hath known the mind of the Lord? or who hath been his counsellor?" (Rom. 11:34). God has no counsellor. The Lord Jesus Christ never called His disciples together and said, "Now, fellows, what do you think I ought to do?" You don't read anything like that in Scripture. The Lord called them together and said, "This is what I am going to do, because this is My Father's will." And Christ has been made unto us wisdom (see 1 Cor. 1:30). Most of us are not very smart. We must go to Him for help.

"The mighty God"—The Hebrew word for this name is *El Gibbor*. He is the one to whom "all power is given." He is the omnipotent God. That little baby lying helpless on Mary's bosom held the universe together. He said, "All power is given unto me in heaven and in earth." He is the Mighty God!

"The everlasting Father"—*Avi-ad*, Father of eternity. This simply means that He is the Creator of all things, even time, the ages, and the far-off purpose of all things. As John said, "All things were made by him; and without him was not any thing made that was made" (John 1:3). In Colossians 1;16 Paul said, "For by him were all things created, that are in heaven, and that are in earth, visible and invisible, whether they be thrones, or dominions, or principalities, or powers: all things were created by him, and for him." Then in Hebrews 1—2 we read, "God. . . . Hath in these last days spoken unto us by his Son, whom he hath appointed heir of all things, by whom also he made the worlds [ages]." The translation of the Greek word *aiōn* should be "ages" instead of "worlds," and that is the thought in this title of His—Father of eternity.

"The Prince of Peace" —*Sar-Shalohim*. There can be no peace on this earth until He is reigning. His government is not static; there is increase and growth. No two days are going to be alike when Jesus is reigning. He is going to occupy the throne of David. This is a literal throne which He will occupy at His second coming. Justice will be dominant in His rule. God's zeal, not man's zany plans, will accomplish this.

THE HELP OF ISRAEL

The remainder of the chapter, verses 8—21, covers the local situation in Isaiah's day and will be partially fulfilled in the immediate future, but it also looks forward to the time of the Great Tribulation for a full and final fulfillment. God will continue to punish this nation and all nations that have turned their backs on Him, until He comes again. Modern men don't like to hear this—they would rather listen to something comforting. Check your history books and see what happened to Israel and other nations who left God out. They have had a sad, sordid story, and I am afraid that you and I live in a nation that is getting ripe for judgment. If we escape, we will be the only nation in the history of the world that has escaped.

CHAPTER 10

THEME: Judgment of Assyria after she executes God's judgment on Israel; the Great Tribulation and Battle of Armageddon

Once again I would like to remind you that this is a series of prophecies which began with chapter 7 and goes through chapter 12. They are prophecies which were given during the reign of Ahaz, a wicked king. On a black background Isaiah gives his predictions, speaking into a local situation, but also he looks down through the ages of time to that day when God is going to set up His kingdom here on earth.

This is another remarkable chapter in God's Word. Great principles and gigantic programs in God's dealings with men and nations are set forth. The chapter opens with a brief discussion on the courts of that day. The injustices of the courts of the nation are reflected in the culture of the people and the chastisement of God.

God will use the Assyrians as we shall see, to judge His people. And Assyria is a symbol of the future "king of the north" who shall come up against Immanuel's land in the last days. This prophecy reaches beyond the immediate future of Isaiah's day and extends down to the last days of the nation Israel. Isaiah identifies the period by the designation, "in that day." The chapter concludes with the awesome picture of the approach of the enemy from the north to the Battle of Armageddon.

UNJUST JUDGES WILL BE JUDGED OF GOD

Woe unto them that decree unrighteous decrees, and that write grievousness which they have prescribed [Isa. 10:1].

"Woe unto them that decree unrighteous decrees"—that is, hand down unrighteous decisions. They should represent justice, but they do not give justice. These first few verses may appear at first to be a discourse of Plato or one of the moralists. The one notable exception is that behind human justice is the justice of God. The judge and throne down here on earth are to reveal His justice and are answerable to Him.

To turn aside the needy from judgment, and to take away the right from the poor of my people, that widows may be their prey, and they may rob the fatherless! [Isa. 10:2].

This verse is very much up-to-date. I think we are seeing the working out of this in our contemporary culture, because the courts are to hand down justice and mirror the justice of God, and they don't. Lawlessness abounds. People sink into degradation. The idea of freedom has been distorted. Every criminal who is arrested ought to be given a fair trial but in order that my family and your family can walk the streets in peace, criminals will have to be punished. Many who are guilty of crimes are set free by a softhearted, softheaded judge. That judge is not giving justice to me and my family or to you and your family.

We hear a lot about justice today, and that is what I want. I want the criminal punished so that I can walk the streets in safety, and so that I can live in my home in safety. In our land it is no longer safe for women to walk on the streets at night. It is not even safe for men in many places. What is the problem? The problem is in our courts—that is where God puts His finger down. The courts are not administering justice.

Now God mentions the poor and the widows and the fatherless; they are the ones who need justice. One of the leading political analysts in this country recently stated on a telecast that every program that has been devised to help the poor has hurt the poor. What is wrong? The only One who will give justice to the poor is God. Judges are supposed to represent God on earth. Today many godless men are judges. They are in no position to judge at all until they recognize that they are representing God.

One of the wonderful things about the founders of our country was the way they believed. Although Thomas Jefferson, for example, was a

free thinker, he had great respect for the Bible. He was not what we
would call a Christian, but he held God's Word in high esteem and
respected the statements made in it. We have gotten so far away from
God and His Word that our courts and government don't even recognize Him. It is a farce to have a man put his hand on the Bible and take
an oath in court of law today, because most judges do not believe it is
the Word of God. The lawyers, the jury, and the men who are taking
the oath probably do not believe it is God's Word. When you don't
believe it, you might as well take an oath on a Sears and Roebuck cata-
log. Some of them may have more respect for that than they do for the
Bible.

God is dealing with principles; and, until a judge represents God,
he cannot represent the people. We have gotten so far from this concept
that I am sure I sound like a square! And that's what I am.

> **And what will ye do in the day of visitation, and in the
> desolation which shall come from far? to whom will ye
> flee for help? and where will ye leave your glory? [Isa.
> 10:3].**

God is saying to the judges, "You are to represent Me, and the day is
coming when I am going to judge *you*." I feel that every judge ought to
recognize the fact that he is one day going to stand before God and give
an account of how he has handled his responsibility here on earth.
Judges in our day seem to have bleeding hearts; they want to show
mercy to the poor criminal. Well, they should be meting out justice to
both rich and poor. In the day of reckoning, the unjust judges will
stand before the Just Judge.

> **Without me they shall bow down under the prisoners,
> and they shall fall under the slain. For all this his anger
> is not turned away, but his hand is stretched out still
> [Isa. 10:4].**

This distortion of justice works itself out in all strata of society. It af-
fects all men and brings about deterioration and degradation. Today we
are at a new low as far as morals are concerned.

JUDGMENT OF ASSYRIA AFTER SHE EXECUTES
GOD'S JUDGMENT ON ISRAEL

Now we come to the key to the entire passage. Here God makes one of the strangest statements in the Bible, and it is too much for a great many folk. My friend, if you don't like it, take your objections to God, because He is the one who said it.

> **O Assyrian, the rod of mine anger, and the staff in their hand is mine indignation [Isa. 10:5].**

This is the key verse of the entire passage, and it sheds light on the whole purpose of God, for this verse says He will use Assyria as a rod to chasten His people Israel. This is an amazing thing. Just as you take up a switch to paddle a little fellow who has done wrong, so God is using Assyria as a switch. He is using Assyria to discipline His people. The destruction which Assyria will wreak is what the hand of the Lord God will wreak. This is difficult for modern man to swallow.

> **I will send him against an hypocritical nation, and against the people of my wrath will I give him a charge, to take the spoil, and to take the prey, and to tread them down like the mire of the streets [Isa. 10:6].**

God goes so far as to say that He is responsible for sending Sennacherib, the Assyrian, against Israel and for sending the northern kingdom of Israel into captivity.

Assyria is a symbol of another kingdom in the north whom God will use in the last days. Many Bible expositors believe this verse has reference to the "beast" which will come out of the sea, mentioned in Revelation 13, who would be the ruler in the Roman Empire. I prefer to be specific and think it is a reference to Russia. Have you noticed that ever since World War II the Russians have won every diplomatic battle? They have won, and they have our country on the ropes today. I wonder if God may not be using them. You might say, "You don't mean that God would use godless Russia?" Well, He used godless Assyria to spank His people in Isaiah's day. God may be using Russia to humiliate us today, and she may have already done that. When we fought in Vietnam, we were not fighting the North Vietnamese; we were fighting Russia. It was a very nice, polite war, and it was embarrassing. It was tragic and horrible. Was God permitting our humiliation in an attempt to bring us to our senses? It didn't seem to work—we have not turned to God.

> **Howbeit he meaneth not so, neither doth his heart think so, but it is in his heart to destroy and cut off nations not a few.**

> **For he saith, Are not my princes altogether kings? [Isa. 10:7–8].**

If you had asked the Assyrian if he was being used as a rod to chasten Israel, he would have laughed at you. If you had asked Russia's dictators if they knew they were rods in the Lord's hands, they would have given you a great ha-ha! They would think such talk was ridiculous. Neither did the Assyrian have any notion that he was prompted of God, nor would he admit it. The Assyrians were having great victories on every hand, and their pride blinded them to their true status. Because they were resting on their own strength and supremacy and were victorious everywhere they turned, they were like Little Jack Horner who sat in a corner, put his thumb in the pie, pulled out a plum, and said, "What a smart boy am I." There are some rulers of nations who are like Little Jack Horner today, but God overrules, though He may be using them to accomplish His purpose.

> **Wherefore it shall come to pass, that when the Lord hath performed his whole work upon mount Zion and on Jerusalem, I will punish the fruit of the stout heart of the king of Assyria, and the glory of his high looks [Isa. 10:12].**

When God gets through using Assyria to punish His people, God will deal with the Assyrians and judge them. They do not escape, either;

history is a testimony to the fact. God judged them. Isaiah shows that God controls and judges all the nations of the earth.

Now He asks a very pointed question:

> **Shall the axe boast itself against him that heweth therewith? or shall the saw magnify itself against him that shaketh it? as if the rod should shake itself against them that lift it up, or as if the staff should lift up itself, as if it were no wood [Isa. 10:15].**

Imagine an axe out in the woods. You are walking through the woods and hear something patting itself on the back and saying, "Look at this big tree I cut down." You walk over to the axe and find nothing but the axe. You say to the axe, "What do you mean, you cut down the tree?" The axe replies, "The tree is down, and I did it." You say that is silly. Somebody had to be using the axe, and that is exactly how it was with Assyria and other nations of the world. God uses nations. That is the reason it is so important today for men in our nation to recognize God, men who look to God for leading and guidance. But we have a divided nation today. In fact, we are lots more divided than we will admit. We have this minority group, that minority group, and the other minority group. However, the real minority is God. Although He is in the minority, Martin Luther said, "One with God is a majority," and if you are with God, you are with the majority. We need to be sure that we are on God's side today, because He is running the universe. As a nation we are a Johnny-come-lately. A two hundred-year-old nation is a baby compared to many of the other nations in history, and we have just about had it. The Assyrians are only instruments in the hand of God.

THE GREAT TRIBULATION AND PRESERVATION OF THE REMNANT

Now we have a vision of the Jewish remnant during the Great Tribulation:

> **And it shall come to pass in that day, that the remnant of Israel, and such as are escaped of the house of Jacob,**

> shall no more again stay upon him that smote them; but
> shall stay upon the LORD, the Holy One of Israel, in truth
> [Isa. 10:20].

In this verse Isaiah begins to look beyond the immediate circumstances which concern the Assyrian to "that day." As we have seen,
"that day" is the day of the Lord, which begins with the Great Tribulation Period.

> Therefore thus saith the Lord God of hosts, O my people
> that dwellest in Zion, be not afraid of the Assyrian: he
> shall smite thee with a rod, and shall lift up his staff
> against thee, after the manner of Egypt [Isa. 10:24].

This is a word of comfort to Judah that she shall be spared from captivity by the Assyrians.

> And it shall come to pass in that day, that his burden
> shall be taken away from off thy shoulder, and his yoke
> from off thy neck, and the yoke shall be destroyed be-
> cause of the anointing [Isa. 10:27].

THE BATTLE OF ARMAGEDDON

Again Isaiah moves beyond, "in that day."

> He is come to Aiath, he is passed to Migron; at Mich-
> mash he hath laid up his carriages:

> They are gone over the passage: they have taken up their
> lodging at Geba; Ramah is afraid; Gibeah of Saul is
> fled.

> Lift up thy voice, O daughter of Gallim: cause it to be
> heard unto Laish, O poor Anathoth.

> Madmenah is removed; the inhabitants of Gebim gather
> themselves to flee.

**As yet shall he remain at Nob that day: he shall shake
his hand against the mount of the daughter of Zion, the
hill of Jerusalem [Isa. 10:28–32].**

This is a remarkable section of prophecy. It gives certain geographical
locations, all of them north of Jerusalem, and it shows the route taken
by Assyria and of the future invader from the north, who I think will
be Russia. The invader comes from the land of Magog (see Ezek. 38–
39).

Now notice the places mentioned: "Aiath" is about fifteen miles
north of Jerusalem. "Migron" is south of Aiath and is the pass where
Jonathan got a victory over the Philistines (see 1 Sam. 14). I understand that General Allenby secured a victory over Turkey in the same
place. "Geba" and "Ramah" are about six miles north of Jerusalem.
"Anathoth" was about three miles north of Jerusalem. This is the home
of the prophet Jeremiah. "Laish" is in the extreme north of Palestine,
in the tribe of Dan. "Madmenah" (dunghill) is a garbage dump north
of Jerusalem. "Gebim" is probably north of Jerusalem. The exact site is
not known. "Nob" is the last place mentioned, and it is north of the
city and in sight of Jerusalem.

This passage clearly charts the march of the enemy from the north,
which brings a state of paralysis and defeat to Jerusalem.

**Behold, the Lord, the LORD of hosts, shall lop the bough
with terror: and the high ones of stature shall be hewn
down, and the haughty shall be humbled [Isa. 10:33].**

God intervenes and delivers His people. I believe this is a reference to
the second coming of Christ to establish His kingdom.

**And he shall cut down the thickets of the forest with
iron, and Lebanon shall fall by a mighty one [Isa.
10:34].**

I believe the "mighty one" is Christ when He comes to the earth.

CHAPTER 11

THEME: The Person and power of the King; the purpose and program of the kingdom

Chapter 11 is a continuation of the prophecy begun in chapter 7 which will conclude with chapter 12. There is progress and development through this section of prophecies which were all given during the reign of Ahaz. In the preceding chapters we have seen a time of judgment, a time that the Lord Jesus called the Great Tribulation Period. Chapter 11 is one of the great messianic prophecies of Scripture. It speaks of the coming of Christ to establish His kingdom and the type of program He will have. In chapter 12 we will have the culmination of this section where we will see the worship of the Lord in the kingdom.

THE PERSON AND POWER OF THE KING

And there shall come forth a rod out of the stem of Jesse, and a Branch shall grow out of his roots [Isa. 11:1].

It is interesting that it says "a rod of the stem of Jesse." David is not mentioned; the one who is mentioned is David's father. Of course that means He is in the line of David, but why does Isaiah go back to Jesse? Well, the royal line did begin with David. Jesse was a farmer, a sheepherder who lived in a little out-of-the-way place called Bethlehem. But by the time of Jesus, the line of David had sunk back to the level of a peasant. It no longer belonged to a prince raised in a palace, but it belonged to One raised in a carpenter shop. Isaiah, therefore, very carefully says that the rod comes "out of the stem of Jesse."

Branch means "a live sprout." This is the second time we have had a reference to the "Branch." The first time it was mentioned was in Isaiah 4:2. There are eighteen words in the Hebrew language translated by our English word *branch*. This is one of the titles given to the Lord Jesus Christ. In Isaiah 53 He is "a root out of a dry ground." Delitzsch, the great Hebrew scholar, wrote, "In the historical fulfillment even the ring of the words of the prophecy is noted: the *nehtzer* (Branch) at first so humble, was a poor *Nazarene*" (see Matt. 2:23). Christ had a humble beginning, born yonder in Bethlehem, a city of David, but a city of Jesse also.

And the spirit of the Lord shall rest upon him, the spirit of wisdom and understanding, the spirit of counsel and might, the spirit of knowledge and of the fear of the Lord [Isa. 11:2].

This is the sevenfold spirit which rested upon the Lord Jesus Christ. The plentitude of power is the sevenfold spirit: (1) of the LORD; (2) of wisdom; (3) of understanding; (4) of counsel; (5) of might; (6) of knowledge; and (7) of the fear of the LORD. The number seven in Scripture does not necessarily mean perfection. The primary thought is fullness, completeness. John 3:34 tells us, ". . . for God giveth not the Spirit by measure unto him." In Ephesians 5:18 we are admonished, ". . . be filled with the Spirit." Some of us just have a few drops at the bottom, others are one fourth filled, and some are half filled. Very few Christians you meet are really *filled* with the Spirit. A little girl once prayed, "Lord, fill me with the Spirit. I can't hold very much, but I can run over a whole lot." Very few Christians are just brimming full, running over on all sides. The Lord Jesus was the exception to that.

1. "The spirit of the Lord shall rest upon him." The Lord Jesus Christ in His humanity went forth in the power of the Spirit. When He comes again, He is going to rule in the power of the Spirit.

2. "The spirit of wisdom." He has been made unto us wisdom (1 Cor. 1:30). He is the only One who can lead and guide you and me through this life. We are no match for the world today. The Lord Jesus Christ could say ". . . for the prince of this world cometh, and hath nothing in me" (John 14:30). Satan cannot find anything in Christ, but he can always find something in us. We need the Spirit of wisdom, and the Lord Jesus Christ is that Spirit of wisdom.

3. "And understanding," which means spiritual discernment. It is distressing to find that so few Christians have any discernment at all. I

am amazed the way some people will follow a certain man purely on a human basis. They like his looks, or the sound of his voice, and they never really comprehend what he is saying, or if what he is saying is true to the Word of God. Christians need the Spirit of understanding. That is one thing for which I have always prayed, and I seem to need it more today than ever before. We need to be aware of who is for the Lord and who isn't.

Not long ago, while driving a car in another city, I was listening to the radio. A man who was preaching blessed my heart, but he went on to say that if he did not get support he would no longer be able to broadcast. I said to myself, "You would think the people in this city would have enough spiritual discernment to support him." He is so much better than many who are being supported. I spoke to a pastor in that city about the man whom I had heard on the radio. He told me that he was a wonderful man, very humble, and a great Bible teacher, but he simply was not getting the support he needed. The Christians in that city need the spirit of understanding. My friend, have you ever prayed for the spirit of understanding? Ask God to give you the understanding that you lack.

4. "The spirit of counsel." All of us need counsel. Did you ever notice that the Lord Jesus Christ never asked anyone for advice? He never asked for counsel; He *gave* it.

5. "Might"—that is, power. Oh, how we need power. Paul says, "That I may know him, and the *power* of his resurrection . . ." (Phil. 3:10, italics mine). We need that today.

6–7. "The spirit of knowledge" and "of the fear of the Lord." I think these come through a study of the Word of God.

THE PURPOSE OF THE KINGDOM

And shall make him of quick understanding in the fear of the Lord: and he shall not judge after the sight of his eyes, neither reprove after the hearing of his ears:

But with righteousness shall he judge the poor, and reprove with equity for the meek of the earth: and he shall

smite the earth with the rod of his mouth, and with the breath of his lips shall he slay the wicked [Isa. 11:3–4].

"The wicked" should be "the wicked one." Satan will have his heyday on earth during the Great Tribulation. There will be no deliverance for the world at that time, humanly speaking. Even Israel will cry out, but help will not come from the north, the south, the east, or the west. Help will come from above. At that time the Messiah will come and establish His kingdom. The reason for the Lord Jesus coming to earth is quite evident: this earth needs a ruler. The world has not voted for Him, and it would not vote for Him, but God has voted for Him. And since this is God's universe, God will establish Him on earth and He is going to judge—not after the sight of His eyes. There won't be a lengthy court case, where, in the end, the criminal is turned loose. The whole thing is rather terrifying: there will be two judgments, one for believers and one for unbelievers. At the beginning of the Tribulation believers will appear before the judgment seat of Christ. Then 1,007 years later there will be the Great White Throne judgment for the lost.

One day I am going to stand before the Lord Jesus Christ. Everything that is phony in my life will be brought out in the open, and so I have been trying to get rid of that which is phony. I want things to be crystal clear, because someday the Lord is going to turn a light on my life and everything will be exposed. What a light that is going to be. It is rather terrifying.

And righteousness shall be the girdle of his loins, and faithfulness the girdle of his reins [Isa. 11:5].

The thing that will gird the Lord's reign will be righteousness and faithfulness. The purpose of the reign of Christ on this earth is to bring in a reign of righteousness and justice as well as to restore the dominion lost by Adam.

THE PARTICULARS OF THE KINGDOM

The wolf also shall dwell with the lamb, and the leopard shall lie down with the kid; and the calf and the young lion and the fatling together; and a little child shall lead them.

And the cow and the bear shall feed; their young ones shall lie down together: and the lion shall eat straw like the ox [Isa. 11:6–7].

During the time when the Lord reigns on earth the calf and the young lion will lie down together. The only way they can lie down together today is if the calf is inside the lion!

"The lion shall eat straw like the ox." That seems ridiculous to us. Anybody knows that a lion does not eat straw. But a Bible teacher, who has a very sharp mind, once said, "I will tell you what I'll do. If you can make a lion, I will make him eat straw." The One who made the lion will be able to make him eat straw when the time comes.

They shall not hurt nor destroy in all my holy mountain; for the earth shall be full of the knowledge of the Lord, as the waters cover the sea [Isa. 11:9].

This kingdom shall extend over the entire earth.

THE PROGRAM OF THE KINGDOM

And in that day there shall be a root of Jesse, which shall stand for an ensign of the people; to it shall the Gentiles seek: and his rest shall be glorious [Isa. 11:10].

The key to this verse is the phrase "in that day." "That day" begins with the Tribulation Period and extends on into the kingdom. The Gentiles shall have a part in the millennial kingdom.

> And it shall come to pass in that day, that the Lord shall set his hand again the second time to recover the remnant of his people, which shall be left, from Assyria, and from Eqypt, and from Pathros, and from Cush, and from Elam, and from Shinar, and from Hamath, and from the islands of the sea [Isa. 11:11].

God shall restore the nation Israel to the land. They were established the first time in the land when Moses led them out of Egypt, and Joshua brought them into the land.

> And he shall set up an ensign for the nations, and shall assemble the outcasts of Israel, and gather together the dispersed of Judah from the four corners of the earth [Isa. 11:12].

What is the "ensign"? That ensign is none other than the Lord Jesus Christ. It will not be some banner that will be lifted up, but He will be the rallying center for the meek of the earth in that day. That will be the day when the meek will inherit the earth. That is God's plan. That is His program, and He will bring it to pass.

> And there shall be an highway for the remnant of his people, which shall be left, from Assyria; like as it was to Israel in the day that he came up out of the land of Egypt [Isa. 11:16].

A great super highway will extend from Assyria to Egypt over the great land bridge of Palestine. Apparently the nations of the world shall come over this to Jerusalem to worship (see Zech. 14:16–18).

CHAPTER 12

THEME: The worship of the Lord in the Millennium; the kingdom age

We have been following a series of prophecies beginning with chapter 7 and concluding with chapter 12. The series began with the judgment of God upon His people. In Isaiah 11 we saw that the kingdom would be established on earth and that the Lord Jesus would reign personally.

Here in chapter 12 we reach a high note. The Tribulation is past, and the storms of life are all over. Now Israel has entered the kingdom, and we find them worshipping and singing praises to God. And we find Israel at the temple, not at the wailing wall. Israel is at the wailing wall today, which is one of the proofs that Israel's return to the land at the present time does not fulfill prophecy.

This brief chapter reads like a psalm—for that is what it is. It is a jewel of beauty. Here is set before us the praise of a people under the direct and personal reign of Christ. It is pure praise from redeemed hearts to God because of His salvation and creation. The curse has been removed from the earth, which is an occasion for praise to God for His display of goodness in creation. You and I have not seen anything like this in nature because of the curse that rests upon it. Today nature has a sharp fang and a bloody claw. During the kingdom age that will change entirely.

PRAISE OF JEHOVAH FOR HIS SALVATION

And in that day thou shalt say, O Lord, I will praise thee: though thou wast angry with me, thine anger is turned away, and thou comfortedst me [Isa. 12:1].

Once again we have the expression "in that day," which marks the beginning of the Great Tribulation Period and goes through the coming of the kingdom that Christ is going to establish upon the earth.

This verse expresses the thought that the night of sin is over and the day of salvation is come. Israel has gone through the terrible night of the Tribulation, and now the light has come. The Tribulation is over, and they enter the peace and joy of the kingdom. This is an occasion for praise! The thing that will characterize the kingdom age is pure joy.

> **Behold, God is my salvation; I will trust, and not be afraid: for the LORD JEHOVAH is my strength and my song; he also is become my salvation [Isa. 12:2].**

Note that they will not say that God *provided* salvation but that He *is* salvation. Salvation is a Person, not a program, or a system, or a ritual, or a liturgy. Salvation is a Person, and that Person is the Lord Jehovah, the Lord Jesus Christ. They are praising Him for His salvation.

> **Therefore with joy shall ye draw water out of the wells of salvation [Isa. 12:3].**

The "wells" speak of abundance. His salvation gives satisfaction and joy to the heart. During the kingdom period there will be a time of great joy, which is what the Lord wants for His own. He wants us to to be happy now. Our salvation should cause us to rejoice and sing praises to the Lord. I do not think we are ever witnesses to Him until we have that joy.

PRAISE OF JEHOVAH FOR HIS CREATION

> **And in that day shall ye say, Praise the LORD, call upon his name, declare his doings among the people, make mention that his name is exalted [Isa. 12:4].**

"In that day," of course, refers to the Millennium, the light part of the day. The "day of the Lord" opened with the night of sin. Our day begins with sunrise, but the day in the Old Testament began with sundown. "Weeping may endure for a night, but joy cometh in the morning" (Ps. 30:5). The time of the Millennium is the morning of joy and the time of thanksgiving to God for salvation—but not only that, it is to thank Him for the fact that He is the Creator. His mighty and expansive "doings" are to be declared among the people, and His name exalted. The "doings" of God include not only His work in creation, but everything He does.

"In that day shall ye say, Praise the LORD"—*hallelujah* is the word.

**Sing unto the LORD; for he hath done excellent things:
this is known in all the earth [Isa. 12:5].**

God has done great things. When the six days of renovation and creation came to an end, God looked upon His work and said that it was good. When God says it is good, it *is* good! I think it would be well for us to thank Him for a perfect salvation and thank Him for creation, even though sin has marred it. In my backyard I notice that the gophers have been burrowing under the fence, and ants get into the house, but in spite of these annoyances there is the singing of the birds and the beauty of the flowers and trees. Even though the earth has been cursed with sin, it is still beautiful. Just think how beautiful it will be when the curse is removed. We will have an occasion to sing praises to God in that day as well as today.

**Cry out and shout, thou inhabitant of Zion: for great is
the Holy One of Israel in the midst of thee [Isa. 12:6].**

This is one great throbbing and pulsating outburst of a redeemed soul who is giving to God all that a poor creature can—his *hallelujah!* We talk of our dedication to God, but we don't even know what dedication means. In that glorious day Israel will know its meaning, and we will too.

CHAPTER 13

THEME: Destruction in the Day of the Lord and in the immediate future

Chapter 13 brings us to an altogether different section. The tone changes immediately. Chapters 13—23 contain "burdens" imposed on nine surrounding nations. A burden is something that you bear, and these burdens are judgments of God upon these nine nations. You could substitute the word *judgment* for "burden" and it would be just as accurate. This is a remarkable passage of Scripture, because most of the prophetic judgments have already been fulfilled. They are now facts of history. Each of these nations had some contact with Israel, and most of them were contiguous to her borders or not very far away. Israel suffered at the hands of some of them—and is suffering today—and will suffer again in the future.

You will find some names in this chapter that are strangely familiar. Egypt is one of them. While some of these judgments will take place in the future, the chief characteristic of this section is that much has been fulfilled and stands today as an evidence of fulfilled prophecy. All of this adds singular interest and importance to these eleven chapters. In this section the Assyrian is no longer the oppressor; another set of nations headed by Babylon takes his place.

It was not pleasant to the prophet to deliver this type of message. This was not the way to win friends and influence people. But God's prophets were not in a popularity contest.

Babylon is the subject of the first burden. It is suggestive of many things to the reverent student of Scripture. First of all, the literal city of Babylon is the primary consideration. This is indeed remarkable, as Babylon in Isaiah's day was an insignificant place. It was not until a century later that Babylon became a world power. God pronounced judgment upon Babylon before it became a nation!

This section does not end with the "burdens" on nine surrounding nations but extends through six woes in chapters 28—33 and con-

cludes with the calm and blessing after the storm in chapters 34 and
35. These last two chapters again give us a millennial picture.

In chapter 13 we will see the punishment of Babylon in the Day of
the Lord. I believe this looks forward to the Great Tribulation Period for
its final fulfillment.

PUNISHMENT OF BABYLON IN THE DAY OF THE LORD

**The burden of Babylon, which Isaiah the son of Amoz
did see [Isa. 13:1].**

The literal city of Babylon in history is in view in this chapter and
also in chapter 14. It became one of the great cities of the ancient
world. In fact, it became the first great world power and is so recognized in Daniel's prophecy. Nebuchadnezzar was the "head of gold" of
Babylon. He was the king of the first great world power.

The city of Babylon will be rebuilt in the future. Babylon is the
symbol of united rebellion against God, which began at the Tower of
Babel and will end in Revelation 17 and 18 where we will see religious
Babylon and political Babylon ruling the world. During the Great Trib-
ulation Period Babylon will go down by a great judgment from God.
This possibly is the first mention of it in Scripture.

**I have commanded my sanctified ones, I have also
called my mighty ones for mine anger, even them that
rejoice in my highness [Isa. 13:3].**

In this verse the word *sanctified* means "set apart for a specific use by
some agency." God says, "I have also called my mighty ones for mine
anger." God has "sanctified" or raised up Babylon for a specific purpose. He did the same thing with Assyria. In Isaiah 10:5 God said
through the prophet Isaiah, "O Assyrian, the rod of mine anger, and
the staff in their hand is mine indignation." God used Assyria to punish His people, and then He judged Assyria. This is what He is going

to do with Babylon. Anything can be sanctified if it is set apart for God. Assyria and Babylon were set aside to punish Israel. They were instruments in His hands for a specific purpose.

> **The noise of a multitude in the mountains, like as of a great people; a tumultuous noise of the kingdoms of nations gathered together: the Lord of hosts mustereth the host of the battle [Isa. 13:4].**

This verse explains what we mean by "sanctified ones." Babylon will come against the southern kingdom of Judah (as Assyria did against the ten northern tribes of Israel) and take it into captivity.

> **They come from a far country, from the end of heaven, even the Lord, and the weapons of his indignation, to destroy the whole land [Isa. 13:5].**

The Babylonians will be the "weapons of his indignation."

> **Howl ye; for the day of the Lord is at hand; it shall come as a destruction from the Almighty [Isa. 13:6].**

This prophecy looks beyond anything that now is in history and projects into the Great Tribulation.

> **Therefore shall all hands be faint, and every man's heart shall melt.**
>
> **And they shall be afraid: pangs and sorrows shall take hold of them; they shall be in pain as a woman that travaileth: they shall be amazed one at another; their faces shall be as flames.**
>
> **Behold, the day of the Lord cometh, cruel both with wrath and fierce anger, to lay the land desolate: and he shall destroy the sinners thereof out of it [Isa. 13:7–9].**

During the Great Tribulation God will again use the power (called Babylon here) to judge these people, just as He did in the past. The Tribulation is spoken of as a time of travail, with men in travail. The Day of the Lord opens with this time of travail.

Now this identifies it as the Great Tribulation:

> **For the stars of heaven and the constellations thereof shall not give their light: the sun shall be darkened in his going forth, and the moon shall not cause her light to shine [Isa. 13:10].**

This is prophesied again by the Lord Jesus in Matthew 24:29: "Immediately after the tribulation of those days shall the sun be darkened, and the moon shall not give her light, and the stars shall fall from heaven, and the powers of the heavens shall be shaken." Revelation 8:12 tells us, "And the fourth angel sounded, and the third part of the sun was smitten, and the third part of the moon, and the third part of the stars; so as the third part of them was darkened, and the day shone not for a third part of it, and the night likewise."

> **And I will punish the world for their evil, and the wicked for their iniquity; and I will cause the arrogancy of the proud to cease, and will lay low the haughtiness of the terrible [Isa. 13:11].**

"I will punish the world for their evil"—We are living in a world today that is moving toward judgment.

> **I will make a man more precious than fine gold; even a man than the golden wedge of Ophir [Isa. 13:12].**

When Christ died for you and me on the cross, that added value to us.

Verses 13–16 go on to tell us that the Tribulation will be a time of worldwide destruction when no "flesh would survive" except for the fact that God will preserve a remnant for Himself.

DESTRUCTION OF BABYLON IN THE DAY OF MAN

Behold, I will stir up the Medes against them, which shall not regard silver; and as for gold, they shall not delight in it [Isa. 13:17].

Who are the Medes? Media and Persia became a dual nation and a mighty empire that conquered Babylon. Isaiah is speaking of that which was going to take place in the immediate future. He identifies those who will destroy Babylon: "the Medes."

And Babylon, the glory of kingdoms, the beauty of the Chaldees' excellency, shall be as when God overthrew Sodom and Gomorrah [Isa. 13:19].

This prophecy has been fulfilled. Babylon was the greatest kingdom that has ever existed upon this earth. The Macedonian empire was great; the Egyptian Empire was great, as was the Roman Empire. At one time Great Britain could have been named a great nation, but I don't think anything can compare to the glory of Babylon. God's Word calls it "the beauty of the Chaldees' excellency," and that excellency God overthrew as He did Sodom and Gomorrah. All you have to do is to look at the ruins of ancient Babylon to recognize that that has happened.

It was a great city that was never rebuilt. Other great cities have been rebuilt. This is especially true of Jerusalem. Rome was destroyed and rebuilt. Cities in Germany were bombed out—absolutely obliterated—and were rebuilt. Frankfurt, Germany, was leveled, and it arose out of the ashes a great city. But Babylon did not arise. God said that it would never again be inhabited. It is true that Babylon will be rebuilt in the future, but not on the ancient site of Babylon. It will be built in a different place.

Babylon represents confusion, and the future Babylon will be a great commercial center, a great religious center, a great political center, a power center, and the educational center of the world again.

> It shall never be inhabited, neither shall it be dwelt in
> from generation to generation: neither shall the Arabian
> pitch tent there; neither shall the shepherds make their
> fold there [Isa. 13:20].

How can Babylon be destroyed and yet appear in the last days as a literal city again? Already the ancient site of the ancient Babylon is seven to nine miles from the Euphrates River. The river ran in a canal right through the ancient city of Babylon. The ancient site will never be rebuilt, but Babylon will be rebuilt on another site. The ruins of ancient Babylon stand as a monument to the accuracy of fulfilled prophecy.

Several archaeologists of the past who have excavated Babylon say that they were never able to get the Arabians to stay in the camp beside the ruins. The Arabians would always go outside the area and stay. They were superstitious. It is interesting that God said they would not pitch their tents in Babylon.

> But wild beasts of the desert shall lie there; and their
> houses shall be full of doleful creatures; and owls shall
> dwell there, and satyrs shall dance there. *demons*
> And the wild beasts of the islands shall cry in their des-
> olate houses, and dragons in their pleasant palaces:
> and her time is near to come, and her days shall not be
> prolonged [Isa. 13:21-22].

"Wild beasts of the desert shall lie there." Lions have been found making their homes amid the ruins.

"Satyrs shall dance there." Satyrs are demons. Satyrs shall dance in Babylon. If you want to go to the dance of the demons, Babylon is the place to go. I hear of folk here in Southern California who worship Satan. One young fellow who claims to belong to a church that worships Satan came to me after a meeting and attacked me in a very vitriolic manner. He insisted that demons are real, and he worshipped them. I agreed that demons are real, but I cautioned him about worshipping them. Then I asked him if he had ever danced with the demons. He looked at me with amazement and said, "No!" So I told him where their dance hall is. I told him that demons dance in the ruins of Babylon. I said to him facetiously, "Why don't you go over there? Brother, if you are going to go halfway, go all the way." Babylon was the headquarters for idolatry in the ancient world. Apparently demons have this spot as a rallying place.

The future Babylon will become a great center on earth. The Man of Sin, the willful king, called the Antichrist, will reign in that place. It will be destroyed just as the ancient Babylon was destroyed. Babylon is a memorial to the fact of the accuracy of fulfilled prophecy and a testimony to the fact that God will also judge the future Babylon.

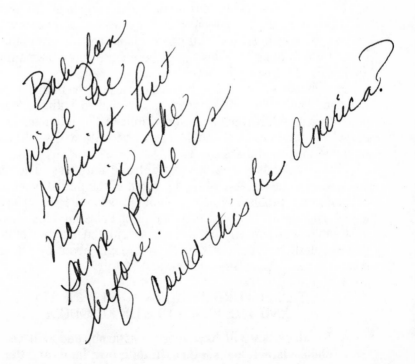

Babylon will be rebuilt but not in the same place as before. Could this be America?

CHAPTER 14

THEME: The millennial kingdom established after the final destruction of Babylon; the origin of evil and its judgment; and the burden of Palestine

This chapter is a continuation of the burden of Babylon begun in chapter 13. The burden of Babylon is actually a judgment on Babylon. Babylon was the first of several nations upon which the judgment of God was to fall. All of the nations to be judged had something to do with Israel—either by physical proximity or political involvement. Great issues are at stake in chapter 14. The origin of evil and its judgment and final removal from this earth is the theme of this section.

Local situations and nations are the expression of these worldwide themes and eternal issues. This chapter looks at nations and the problems of life through the telescope rather than placing them under the microscope for inspection.

This chapter opens on a joyful note because of the final judgment of Babylon. The millennial kingdom is established with all fears and dangers removed. No enemy of God is abroad. The judgment here and elsewhere in this Book of Isaiah is explained. We will see here God's plan and purpose for the earth.

This chapter is a mixture of light and darkness. The chapter changes from the ecstasy of the kingdom to the punishment of hell. Satan and the problem of evil are brought before us. There is an extended section on the final destruction of Babylon. This chapter of great subjects and strong contrasts closes with the insertion of the burden of Palestine, which was probably brought about by the sudden demise of King Ahaz (see 2 Kings 16:19–20).

THE FUTURE RESTORATION OF ISRAEL AND THE PEACE OF THE KINGDOM

For the LORD will have mercy on Jacob, and will yet choose Israel, and set them in their own land: and the

**strangers shall be joined with them, and they shall
cleave to the house of Jacob [Isa. 14:1].**

This verse reaches down to the end times. God has said again and
again that the nation Israel will be restored to her land. Now I do not
think you see fulfillment of the prophecies there today. When God re-
stores them to the land, Israel will not have any problems with other
nations. They won't need to turn to Russia, or the United States, or to
the United Nations for help. The Lord Jesus will reign there.

There are many people who say they believe in the verbal, plenary
inspiration of the Scriptures, but they will turn right around and say
that this passage is not literal. When you deny its reality and the fact
that it is literal, you deny the inspiration of Scripture. "For the LORD
will have mercy on Jacob, and will yet choose Israel"—He has said
that too many times for anyone to say, "I didn't quite get it." Or, "It
means something else."

**And the people shall take them, and bring them to their
place: and the house of Israel shall possess them in the
land of the LORD for servants and handmaids: and they
shall take them captives, whose captives they were; and
they shall rule over their oppressors [Isa. 14:2].**

My friend, this has not yet been fulfilled. "The people" in this verse
are Gentiles. The Gentiles are going to return them to Palestine. But
the Gentiles up to this point have actually hindered them. Even Great
Britain, when they had a mandate in the land, would not let the Jews
return after World War II. But the Jews went in anyway, because they
had to go somewhere. How the multitudes went to that land is a real
saga of suffering. As I write, Russia is hindering the Jews from return-
ing to Palestine. Other nations are not concerned for them either. Now
the Jews throughout the world are interested in helping their brethren
return to the land, but Gentiles are not helping them. I take it, therefore, that we are not seeing the fulfillment of Scripture.

**And it shall come to pass in the day that the LORD shall
give thee rest from thy sorrow, and from thy fear, and**

**from the hard bondage wherein thou wast made to serve
[Isa. 14:3].**

The Jews have sorrow in that land today, and they are in fear. I walked
through the streets of Jerusalem and through the streets of some other
cities in Palestine some time ago, and there were soldiers everywhere.
Why? The nation is fearful. Even if things were settled, they would
still be in fear. There is no rest from sorrow for them.

**That thou shalt take up this proverb against the king of
Babylon, and say, How hath the oppressor ceased! the
golden city ceased! [Isa. 14:4].**

I think "Babylon," in this passage, represents the great enemy in the
last days who will be headquartered in Babylon. It represents all the
enemies of Israel. Babylon was an inveterate hater of this nation.

**The LORD hath broken the staff of the wicked, and the
sceptre of the rulers.**

**He who smote the people in wrath with a continual
stroke, he that ruled the nations in anger, is persecuted,
and none hindereth [Isa. 14:5-6].**

These verses speak of the final judgment at the end of the Great Tribulation Period. Judgment has to take place. This earth must be judged.
There is too much injustice here. Someone is going to have to handle
the judgment, and I thank the Lord that it won't be me. I am thankful that we don't have to look to men in these matters. The Lord Jesus
will do the judging.

**The whole earth is at rest, and is quiet: they break forth
into singing.**

**Yea, the fir trees rejoice at thee, and the cedars of Leba-
non, saying, Since thou art laid down, no feller is come
up against us [Isa. 14:7-8].**

What is described in this passage has not yet taken place. After the war of Armageddon and the coming of Christ, rest and peace come to the earth. Instead of sorrow there is singing. Weeping is only for the night. The morn of joy has come. *Rev 17 + 18*

THE FINAL RULER OF THE WORLD
CAST INTO SHEOL

Hell from beneath is moved for thee to meet thee at thy coming: it stirreth up the dead for thee, even all the chief ones of the earth; it hath raised up from their thrones all the kings of the nations [Isa. 14:9].

"Hell," in this verse, is *Sheol*. It can mean the grave or the place of torment. Evidently the latter meaning is in view here.

All they shall speak and say unto thee, Art thou also become weak as we? art thou become like unto us?

Thy pomp is brought down to the grave, and the noise of thy viols: the worm is spread under thee, and the worms cover thee [Isa. 14:10-11].

All the pomp and glory of man is removed.

THE ORIGIN OF SATAN AND EVIL

How art thou fallen from heaven, O Lucifer, son of the morning! how art thou cut down to the ground, which didst weaken the nations! [Isa. 14:12].

"Lucifer" is none other than Satan. Lucifer, according to Ezekiel 28, *: 11-19* is the highest creature that God ever created. But he was a Judas Iscariot—he turned on God. He set his will over God's will. In Luke 10:18 the Lord Jesus says, ". . . I beheld Satan as lightning fall from heaven." In 1 John 3:8 we are told, "He that committeth sin is of the devil; for the devil sinneth from the beginning. For this purpose the Son of God was manifested, that he might destroy the works of the devil." Then in Revelation 12:7–9 we are told, "And there was war in heaven: Michael and his angels fought against the dragon; and the dragon fought and his angels, And prevailed not; neither was their place found any more in heaven. And the great dragon was cast out, that old serpent, called the Devil, and Satan, which deceiveth the whole world: he was cast out into the earth, and his angels were cast out with him." This is a picture of this creature Lucifer at the very beginning.

What was the sin of this creature created higher than any other? Well, what is sin in its final analysis? I'm not speaking philosophically, but theologically—what is sin?

> **For thou hast said in thine heart, I will ascend into heaven, I will exalt my throne above the stars of God: I will sit also upon the mount of the congregation, in the sides of the north:**
>
> **I will ascend above the heights of the clouds; I will be like the most High [Isa. 14:13–14].**

These are the five "I wills" of Lucifer. He was setting his will over against the will of God. This is sin in embryo. This is the evolution of evil. There is no evolution of man, but there is evolution of sin. It began by a creature setting his will against the will of God. As a free moral agent, the creature must be allowed to do this. It is nonsense to talk about a creature who has a free moral will, who can do anything he wants to, but is restricted in his movements in a certain area. Lucifer had a free will.

This is man's original sin: "All we like sheep have gone astray; we have turned every one to his own way; and the Lord hath laid on him the iniquity of us all" (Isa. 53:6). Murder is sin, not just because God says it is, but because it is contrary to the will and character of God. Anything that is contrary to the character and will of God is sin, regardless of what it is. I think that some people can even displease God by going to church.

Imagine little bitty puffed-up creature man, who says to God, "I won't do what You want me to do. I am going to do it my way" That is exactly what man is saying today. Well, friend, you are *not* going to do things your way because God's will is going to prevail in the final analysis. Therefore, the prayer of all God's people should be, ". . . Thy will be done in earth, as it is in heaven" (Matt. 6:10). Anything contrary to His will is sin, regardless of what it is.

The sin of Satan was overweening pride. He did not go out and get drunk, and he didn't steal anything. He went against God's will. He was created as an angel of light; he was the "son of the morning," a perfect being. He was given a free moral will—he could choose what he wanted. But he was lifted up—so lifted up by pride that he set his will against the will of God. It wasn't the purpose of Satan to be different from God; he wanted to be like God. In other words, he wanted *to be God*. He put his will above the will of God, and any creature who does that puts himself in the place of God.

There are many men like Lucifer today. They put their wills above the will of God and take His place. That is what sin is all about in the human family. There are only two ways: God's way and man's way. That is what the Lord Jesus Christ meant when He said, ". . . I am the way, the truth, and the life: no man cometh unto the Father, but by me" (John 14:6). My friend, you live in God's universe today. You breathe His air and enjoy His sunshine. He never sends you a bill for either one or for the life He furnishes. You are His creature. You owe Him a great deal. You are to obey Him.

In his natural state, man is unable to obey God; that is why we have to come to Him through the Lord Jesus Christ as lost sinners. Then we are given a new nature. That is what it means to be born again.

Yet thou shalt be brought down to hell, to the sides of the pit.

They that see thee shall narrowly look upon thee, and consider thee, saying, Is this the man that made the earth to tremble, that did shake kingdoms;

> That made the world as a wilderness, and destroyed the
> cities thereof; that opened not the house of his pris-
> oners? [Isa. 14:15–17].

God is yet going to judge Satan, and that judgment will be severe.
Satan is finally going to be cast into the lake of fire which was prepared for him.

God is working out a great plan and purpose that is far beyond the
thinking of anyone here on this earth. It is not for you and me to question it. Rather, we need to trust Him, because He is prepared to extend
to us mercy, grace, and love.

THE FUTURE REBELLION OF BABYLON

> All the kings of the nations, even all of them, lie in glory,
> every one in his own house [Isa. 14:18].

Babylon was controlled by Satan. You remember that Satan offered to
the Lord Jesus the kingdoms of this world (see Luke 4:5–7). Babylon
belonged to him. Back of Babylon and all the kingdoms of this world is
Satan. In the future, Babylon will evidently become the rallying point
for all the nations which are against God.

> For I will rise up against them, saith the LORD of hosts
> and cut off from Babylon the name, and remnant, and
> son, and nephew, saith the LORD.

> I will also make it a possession for the bittern, and pools
> of water: and I will sweep it with the besom of destruc-
> tion, saith the LORD of hosts [Isa. 14:22–23].

If you have ever seen pictures of the ruins of Babylon, you realize how
literally these verses have been fulfilled. In the future, Babylon will be
rebuilt (though at a different site). It will once again be a place of world
rulership, and it will be a Tower of Babel lifted against God. And
again God will come down to judge, and that will be the final judg-

ment. The reason that these great truths have been given to us is so that
we will know what is coming in the future.

> The LORD of hosts hath sworn, saying, Surely as I have
> thought, so shall it come to pass; and as I have pur-
> posed, so shall it stand:

> That I will break the Assyrian in my land, and upon my
> mountains tread him under foot: then shall his yoke de-
> part from off them, and his burden depart from off their
> shoulders [Isa. 14:24–25].

"The Assyrian" represents the king that is coming from the north.

Verses 19–27 give a detailed account of the coming judgment of
Babylon and all that it represents. It has been only partially fulfilled in
the past, but it has been fulfilled quite literally.

THE FIERCE REPUDIATION OF PALESTINE

> In the year that king Ahaz died was this burden [Isa.
> 14:28].

There is inserted at this point the burden of Palestine which was pre-
cipitated by the death of Ahaz. Ahaz had reigned for sixteen years and
had been an evil king. The people felt he would be followed by an evil
king, but they were delighted to be rid of him. There was a bare possibility that a good king might follow him—and they did get one, by the
way.

> Rejoice not thou, whole Palestina, because the rod of
> him that smote thee is broken: for out of the serpent's
> root shall come forth a cockatrice, and his fruit shall be
> a fiery flying serpent [Isa. 14:29].

Two more good kings ruled after Ahaz, but the worst kings are yet to
come. The people are to understand that just the rule of man will not

bring about improvement in the world. In this country we seem to feel that if we change presidents or parties there is going to be an improvement. We have done that, and there has been no improvement. God tells Palestine not to rejoice just because Ahaz is dead. Things are not going to get any better at all.

Before the kingdom blessings prevail, there will be a severe judgment of God upon that land. It will be more severe than that of the surrounding nations, because this nation had light, and light creates responsibility. Isaiah is looking into the future when there will be the Great Tribulation Period and the Antichrist's rule.

There are those who do not feel that the burden mentioned here is much of a burden but it is called a burden, and it is about Palestina. The name *Palestina* is quite interesting. It refers to those who gave that name to the land, the Philistines. They had come up the coast of Egypt, and they slipped into the land. They were there when Israel arrived. Apparently the Philistines had not been in the land during the days of Abraham, because the Canaanites were then in the land. But when the children of Israel returned four hundred years later, the Philistines had come into the land. In the Books of Zephaniah and Zechariah are specific prophecies against Ashdod and Ashkelon, two Philistine cities. They were to be destroyed, and it was literally fulfilled. Verses 30-32 describe the judgment in detail, and it is fierce!

CHAPTERS 15 AND 16

THEME: The burden of Moab

This brief chapter records the third burden, the burden of Moab. Chapters 15 and 16 deal with Moab. This seems strange in light of the fact that there were only two chapters that dealt with Babylon, and Babylon was the first great world power. Compared to Babylon, Moab may seem to us like it was very small potatoes. But in Isaiah's day—in fact, as early as the time of David—this land was very important, and it was a great kingdom.

Moab was the nation which came from Lot through the incestuous relationship with his elder daughter. Moab, the illegitimate son of this sordid affair, was the father of the Moabites. These people became the inveterate and persistent enemies of the nation of Israel. Balak, their king, hired Balaam, the prophet, to curse Israel, for he feared them when they passed through the land of Moab.

The lovely story told in the Book of Ruth concerns a maid of Moab. This maiden of Moab was a very wonderful person. I am in love with Ruth and have been for a long time—not only the Book of Ruth, but also with my wife whose name is Ruth. David was part Moabite for his father Jesse was a descendant of Obed, the son of Boaz and Ruth. David had relatives in Moab, and he took his father and mother there when Saul was pursuing him.

Today the nation of Moab has disappeared, but who are the modern Moabites? I feel that Moab is representative of those who make a profession of being children of God but actually have no vital relationship with Him (see Heb. 12:8). Like Felix and Festus, the Moabites were "almost persuaded." They were not very far from the kingdom, but they never quite made it. They were neighbors of God's people but never became followers of God.

The modern "Moabite" is easily discovered. He is in our churches today. He parades as a Christian. He is the one Paul describes in 2 Timothy 3:5: "having a form of godliness, but denying the power thereof: from such turn away." Jude 16 also describes him: "These are murmurers, complainers, walking after their own lusts; and their mouth speaketh great swelling words, having men's persons in admiration because of advantage." The modern Moabites are ungodly. They pretend to be godly, but they are not. They flatter you with great swelling words when they think they can get something from you, but drop you the minute they find that they cannot get anything from you.

Moab was a dangerous friend to have. It was never a trusted ally of Israel.

THE SUDDEN DESTRUCTION OF MOAB

The burden of Moab. Because in the night Ar of Moab is laid waste, and brought to silence; because in the night Kir of Moab is laid waste, and brought to silence [Isa. 15:1].

"In the night"—the burden of Moab came suddenly. This expression is repeated twice to emphasize the suddenness of the storm which struck the nation. The storm came at night, and their night of weeping never ended. Assyria destroyed this nation in a way that is unbelievable and almost unspeakable. They seemed to wipe Moab off the face of the earth.

"Kir" is Kerak on a mountain peak about ten miles from the southeast corner of the Dead Sea.

He is gone up to Bajith, and to Dibon, the high places, to weep: Moab shall howl over Nebo, and over Medeba: on all their heads shall be baldness, and every beard cut off [Isa. 15:2].

There are several places mentioned in this verse with which I do not think we are acquainted. "Bajith" means house and apparently refers to the temple of Chemosh which was in that land. "Dibon" was a town on the east side of Jordan where the Moabite stone was found. "Nebo" is the mountain from which Moses saw the Promised Land. "Medeba" was a city that belonged to Reuben (see Josh. 13:16).

All of these cities and places belonged to Moab during Isaiah's day. They were going to be destroyed because, although the Moabites professed to know God, they spent their time in heathen temples dedicated to pagan gods, saying that they were worshipping the living and true God.

> **In their streets they shall gird themselves with sackcloth: on the tops of their houses, and in their streets, every one shall howl, weeping abundantly [Isa. 15:3].**

When I was in Amman, Jordan, I had a very funny feeling. It is a weird sort of place. It is a very poor land now, but in Isaiah's day it was a rich country. I felt as if the judgment of God was still on that place.

THE SYMPATHY OF THE PROPHET FOR ZOAR

The judgment upon Moab was so serious that even Isaiah was moved:

> **My heart shall cry out for Moab; his fugitives shall flee unto Zoar, an heifer of three years old: for by the mounting up of Luhith with weeping shall they go it up; for in the way of Horonaim they shall raise up a cry of destruction [Isa. 15:5].**

Although Moab was the enemy of Israel, Isaiah's heart goes out to them in sympathy because of the terror that has come upon them. This reveals the heart of God. In spite of people's sin today, God still loves them and will extend His mercy to them if they will but turn to Him.

The rest of the chapter gives a detailed description of the further ravaging of the land of Moab. It has been literally fulfilled.

THE FINAL OVERTURE OF MERCY
OFFERED TO MOAB

Chapter 16 opens with a last call to Moab to avail herself of the mercy of God which He has provided for her.

> **Send ye the lamb to the ruler of the land from Sela to the wilderness, unto the mount of the daughter of Zion [Isa. 16:1].**

A lamb was to be sent from Moab to Israel for an offering on the altar there. The lamb was the animal of sacrifice which best depicts Christ, ". . . the Lamb of God, which taketh away the sin of the world" (John 1:29). If they sent a lamb, Moab would signify that they recognized the God of Israel. They did not send a lamb. The Moabites wanted to be religious without acknowledging the fact that they were subject to a higher will and were sinners in the sight of God. This was their great sin.

> **For it shall be, that, as a wandering bird cast out of the nest, so the daughters of Moab shall be at the fords of Arnon [Isa. 16:2].**

I crossed that little river of Arnon. It is not much of a river, and it certainly could not separate the Moabites from the Assyrians. They were taken there.

> **And in mercy shall the throne be established: and he shall sit upon it in truth in the tabernacle of David, judging, and seeking judgment, and hasting righteousness [Isa. 16:5].**

In Acts 15:16 James mentions that the "tabernacle of David" is "fallen down," but that after God has called out the Gentiles to form the church, He will turn again and rebuild the tabernacle of David. This is what Isaiah is talking about here.

THE FIERCE PRIDE OF MOAB

We have heard of the pride of Moab; he is very proud:
even of his haughtiness, and his pride, and his wrath:
but his lies shall not be so [Isa. 16:6].

trusting himself not God

The reason that God had to reject and judge Moab was that their pride
had led them to reject God's proffered offer of mercy. God would have
delivered them, but instead they trusted in their own righteousness.

THE FULFILLMENT OF JUDGMENT
WITHIN THREE YEARS

This is the word that the LORD hath spoken concerning
Moab since that time.

But now the LORD hath spoken, saying, Within three
years, as the years of an hireling, and the glory of
Moab shall be contemned, with all that great multitude;
and the remnant shall be very small and feeble [Isa.
16:13–14].

When God deals with the nations that have to do with Israel, He uses
a calendar. He never uses a calendar with the church. Within three
years the Moabites were to be destroyed, and within three years God
used Assyria to destroy this nation. It was the judgment of God upon
them because of their pride.

Lucifer, the son of the morning, was also lifted up with pride. He
wanted to lift his throne above the throne of God. He wanted to establish his own self-contained kingdom and be independent of God. Basically, this is the position of all liberal theology. Pride is the thing that
causes people to reject God's Word and His revelation. Most people
want a do-it-yourself religion. They want to *do something* to be saved,
because it ministers to their pride. Many accuse church members of
being hypocritical, selfish, and some actually anti-God. All this rests
basically on the pride of the human heart: "we have turned every one
to his own way" (Isa. 53:6).

Judgment came upon Moab. This out-of-the-way nation, entirely
forgotten today, has had a message for us.

CHAPTERS 17 AND 18

THEME: The burden of Damascus and Ephraim; the burden of the land beyond the rivers of Ethiopia

THE BURDEN OF DAMASCUS AND EPHRAIM

Damascus was the leading city of Syria, and it still is that today. Many have called it the oldest city in the world. There are, of course, several places that make the same claim. In Greece, the city of Mycenae claims to be the oldest, but there is not much there today except a very good Greek restaurant! By the Jordan there is a sign giving the kilometers to "Jericho, The World's Oldest City." I guess about every country in the world claims to have the oldest city. I have been waiting for my native state of Texas to make the same claim—I am sure they will dig it up some day. However, Damascus does have a good claim to it. It was Vitringa who wrote, "Damascus has been destroyed oftener than any other town . . .it rises again from ashes." But "Damascus" in this chapter refers to the entire nation of Syria.

Ephraim is the name of a tribe of Israel, it is the name of a city, it is the name of a mountain, and it is the name of a man. *Ephraim* is often used in Scripture to refer to the ten northern tribes of Israel. The prophets used it in that way: "For Israel slideth back as a backsliding heifer. . . .Ephraim is joined to idols . . ." (Hos. 4:16–17).

Therefore, we have here in Chapter 17 the burden of Damascus and Ephraim, or in other words, the burden of the nations of Syria and Israel. Because of the confederacy between Syria and Israel (often for the purpose of coming against Judah), Israel is linked with the judgments pronounced on Syria. Partners in crime means partners in judgment.

> **The burden of Damascus. Behold, Damascus is taken away from being a city, and it shall be a ruinous heap [Isa. 17:1].**

"It shall be a ruinous heap"—there will be those quick to point out that this has not been fulfilled, inasmuch as the present-day city of Damascus claims to be the same as the original city. As I have said before, there is a far-off fulfillment of all these prophecies and a local or contemporary fulfillment also. There are two possible explanations for the problem presented by this prophecy:

1. Historians are not always accurate in their identification of such things as the locations of ancient cities. One man wrote a profound history not long ago and then made the statement that the biggest liars in the world have been historians. In the area of present-day Damascus there happen to be many ruins of a city, and any one of these ruins could be the original Damascus. Damascus is like a great many of the ancient cities in that when it was destroyed in one place, they did not always rebuild on the same site, but shifted it somewhat to another location. (Other cities, such as the sacred city of Jerusalem, were rebuilt on exactly the same site because of the significance of the location to the people.) We will just leave this problem to the archaeologist who hasn't come up with the answer yet as to which of the ruins is old Damascus.

2. Damascus has withstood the ravages of war throughout history and has never ceased being a city, although it has shifted locations. It probably is the oldest city in the world. It thus far has survived every catastrophe that has come upon the earth, particularly in a land that has seen army after army march through it. But it will not survive during the Great Tribulation Period. It will be destroyed; and, as Isaiah says here, it will cease being a city. It will become a ruinous heap.

Both of these explanations show the accuracy of the prophecy that Isaiah gives here.

> **The cities of Aroer are forsaken: they shall be for flocks, which shall lie down, and none shall make them afraid [Isa. 17:2].**

"The cities of Aroer" is a surburban area near Damascus. This entire area would be destroyed. This probably has happened in the past, and it will happen again.

> The fortress also shall cease from Ephraim, and the
> kingdom from Damascus, and the remnant of Syria:
> they shall be as the glory of the children of Israel, saith
> the LORD of hosts [Isa. 17:3].

The northern kingdom of Israel must bear her share of the burden or
judgment of Damascus because of the alliance they have. Both were
besieged by Tiglath-pileser, as recorded in 2 Kings 15:29, and were
finally deported by the Assyrian, Shalmaneser, as recorded in 2 Kings
17:6. This certainly was a partial fulfillment of Isaiah's prophecy;
and, as far as many are concerned, it is the total fulfillment. But I feel
that all of this is looking even to a future day. Certainly this has been
fulfilled partially at least, but oftentimes in the Word of God we find
that God is letting us know by giving an earlier partial fulfillment, that
a prophecy will be completely fulfilled.

In the remainder of this chapter we find that the judgment is going
to be carried out. I will not go into much detail here.

> Because thou hast forgotten the god of thy salvation, and
> hast not been mindful of the rock of thy strength, there-
> fore shalt thou plant pleasant plants, and shalt set it
> with strange slips [Isa. 17:10].

Isaiah is talking to the northern kingdom of Israel, and what he says
has been literally fulfilled. It has its spiritual application also, as all of
this does. The land of Israel in our day has been planted with pleasant
plants and slips. I had the privilege personally of setting out five trees
in Israel. The forests of the cedars of Lebanon have almost been removed, but there are many trees in that land. The Mount of Olives was
covered with trees, but while the Turks controlled Palestine, practically all the land was denuded of its greenery. After World War I England began a movement to plant trees in that land, and the present
government of Israel has continued this policy, so that literally millions of trees have been set out.

THE BURDEN OF THE LAND BEYOND
THE RIVERS OF ETHIOPIA

Chapter 18 deals with the fifth burden, that of the land "beyond the rivers of Ethiopia." The exact nation that Isaiah had in mind has not been clearly established, so there have been many interpretations. Some have thought that he is talking about Egypt, but the description does not fit that country. Also, Egypt is the subject of the next chapter, where we see that God is not through with that kingdom. Prophecy literally has been fulfilled concerning her. Those who say that chapter 18 is referring to England and the United States weary me with that interpretation. I feel like yawning, as that is certainly not sound interpretation of the Word of God!

I believe that Ethiopia best suits the text and tenor of Scripture. But which Ethiopia is intended? There are two mentioned in Scripture. The word for Ethiopia is Cush. There is one in Asia (see Gen. 2:13), and there is one in Africa. I believe we are talking about the Ethiopia that is in Africa. It is the land "beyond the rivers," and the rivers of Ethiopia are the Nile River.

Now God calls the world's attention to Ethiopia:

Woe to the land shadowing with wings, which is beyond the rivers of Ethiopia [Isa. 18:1].

"Woe" is an unfortunate translation. Actually, it is the same word that is translated as "ah" in Isaiah 1:4, where it is a sigh, or as "ho" in Isaiah 55, where it is a form of address that demands attention. Here God is saying, "Ho, to the land—Hear Me, listen to this!"

"Shadowing with wings" might better be translated "rustling with wings." This is quite interesting. A missionary to the land for quite some years told me that Ethiopia is noted for its birds. It is called "the land of wings." This helps to confirm that the land in question here is Ethiopia.

> That sendeth ambassadors by the sea, even in vessels of
> bulrushes upon the waters, saying, Go, ye swift messen-
> gers, to a nation scattered and peeled, to a people terri-
> ble from their beginning hitherto; a nation meted out
> and trodden down, whose land the rivers have spoiled!
> [Isa. 18:2].

Some have held this sea power to be England or the United States, but
"vessels of bulrushes" would not characterize the boats of any modern
nation! Dr. F. C. Jennings, in his profound work on Isaiah, makes a
good case for the steamboat, but since modern ships use oil, this
seems to have no place in our day.

"A nation scattered and peeled" is Israel. This is patently evident,
and most of the sound students of the Word of God concur in this.

> All ye inhabitants of the world, and dwellers on the
> earth, see ye, when he lifted up an ensign on the moun-
> tains; and when he bloweth a trumpet, hear ye [Isa.
> 18:3].

Many students of the Word consider the "ensign" mentioned here to be
the ark of the tabernacle, which was later transferred to the temple. It
disappeared at the time of the Babylonian captivity, and there is a tradition which says it was carried to Ethiopia. I have been told that there
is a church in that land that claims to have the ark. I don't know if that
is true or not, but an ensign will come out of that land.

> In that time shall the present be brought unto the Lord of
> hosts of a people scattered and peeled, and from a peo-
> ple terrible from their beginning hitherto; a nation
> meted out and trodden under foot, whose land the rivers
> have spoiled, to the place of the name of the Lord of
> hosts, the mount Zion [Isa. 18:7].

This is evidently a reference to the time when the kingdom of Christ
will be established on this earth and the Ethiopians will come again to

Jerusalem to worship. There is no judgment spoken against them. In Psalm 87:4, evidently in reply to what he is doing in Jerusalem, the Ethiopian answers that he was born there. God has wonderful things to say about Ethiopia!

CHAPTERS 19 AND 20

THEME: The burden of Egypt—through gloom to glory

Chapters 13—23 present eleven judgments against nations that surrounded the nation Israel. The burden of Egypt is the sixth burden. Egypt is certainly one nation we would expect to find on this list. This is one of the greatest passages that illustrate the accuracy of the Word of God. Certainly fulfilled prophecy is proof that the Bible is the Word of God. No nation figures more prominently on the pages of Scripture than Egypt in its relationship to Israel. Egypt has a longer history than any other nation mentioned in Scripture, including Israel. In fact, it was down in the land of Egypt that the nation Israel was born. Seventy souls from the family of Jacob journeyed there, and four hundred years later they left Egypt with at least a million and a half people. Egypt was an old nation at that time. It has had a continuous history right down to the present day. It is in existence today and plays a prominent part in world events. And it has a glorious future predicted in this chapter. This chapter contains all the elements which enter into the history of the nation—its past, present, and future.

Egypt came into prominence early in Scripture when Abraham ran away to Egypt and got into difficulties. Later Joseph was sold into Egypt, and during a famine Jacob and his sons went down into Egypt with their families. There Israel became a great nation as slaves in the brickyards. Later on, after the children of Israel returned to the Promised Land, two of their kings, Ahaz and Hezekiah, made an alliance with Egypt and found her an unreliable ally.

During the intertestamental period, between Malachi and Matthew, Israel suffered grievously at the hand of Egypt. When the Lord Jesus Christ was born, He was taken down into Egypt. The gospel made many converts in Egypt during the first three centuries of the Christian era. Out of that section of North Africa came three great saints of the church—Athanasius, Origen, and Augustine—and others also. In our day, Egypt has been a thorn in the side of the new nation of Israel.

FULFILLED PROPHECY CONCERNING EGYPT

The burden of Egypt. Behold, the LORD rideth upon a swift cloud, and shall come into Egypt: and the idols of Egypt shall be moved at his presence, and the heart of Egypt shall melt in the midst of it [Isa. 19:1].

The idolatry of Egypt is the chief target of God's condemnation. We will pick up this theme again when we get to the Book of Ezekiel where God says that every idol would disappear from Egypt. Perhaps no people were ever given over to idolatry more than the Egyptians, with the possible exception of Babylon, which was the fountainhead of idolatry. What Paul said in Romans 1:21–23 fits Egypt like a glove: "Because that, when they knew God, they glorified him not as God, neither were thankful; but became vain in their imaginations, and their foolish heart was darkened. Professing themselves to be wise, they became fools, And changed the glory of the uncorruptible God into an image made like to corruptible man, and to birds, and four-footed beasts, and creeping things."

History bears testimony to the fact that Egypt was originally monotheistic, that is, they worshipped one God; but they gradually lapsed into the basest sort of idolatry where every creature under heaven was worshiped, including the bull, the frog, the scarab (a bug), the fish, and all sorts of birds. When Moses was ready to deliver the children of Israel from Egypt, God had to carry on warfare, which I call the battle of the gods, in which God through Moses brought down plagues upon Egypt. Jehovah struck at all forms of idolatry in Egypt—from the sun in the heavens and the River Nile to frogs and lice in the land. Each plague was directed against one of the gods or idols of Egypt.

Now God comes down again in a cloud like a chariot to destroy the idols of Egypt. It is interesting to know that idolatry has long since disappeared from the land, though the people dwell in the ignorance and superstition of the Moslem religion. I have visited Egypt twice, and there is no darkness like the darkness in the land of Egypt. Isaiah's prophecy has been fulfilled.

And I will set the Egyptians against the Egyptians: and
they shall fight every one against his brother, and every
one against his neighbour; city against city, and kingdom against kingdom [Isa. 19:2].

At about the time of Isaiah several pharaohs arose who could no longer
control this great kingdom, and the army no longer obeyed them. The
people no longer respected the government. This caused the setting
up of weak city-states that were self-governing for a period of time. For
this reason there were great cities such as Thebes and Karnak in Upper
Egypt, and in Lower Egypt there was another cluster of great cities.
There was a break-up of cities also at Memphis, known in Scripture as
Noph.

And the spirit of Egypt shall fail in the midst thereof;
and I will destroy the counsel thereof: and they shall
seek to the idols, and to the charmers, and to them that
have familiar spirits and to the wizards [Isa. 19:3].

The proud nation of Egypt had advanced its civilization much further
than other nations. There is not a nation under the sun today that does
not owe a great deal to the civilization of Egypt. There came a time
when Egypt turned to idols and finally in desperation resorted to spir-
itism. You find that at the time of Moses, for instance, the magicians
who were called in could actually duplicate some of the miracles that
Moses did. The time came when they could no longer duplicate what
Moses did, but what they did at first reveals the fact that they were not
fakers; they actually had satanic powers.

"The spirit of Egypt shall fail." The time came when the nation was
brought down to a low level.

And the Egyptians will I give over into the hand of a
cruel lord; and a fierce king shall rule over them, saith
the Lord, the Lord of hosts [Isa. 19:4].

This "cruel lord" cannot be positively identified from history, as Egypt was attacked and subdued by a series of invaders who eventually reduced the nation to poverty.

And the waters shall fail from the sea, and the river shall be wasted and dried up [Isa. 19:5].

The "sea" in this verse refers to the River Nile which was the main artery of the nation and a large body of water. "The rivers" are the canals that were built especially at the mouth of the river. That delta area had to be kept open in that day because so much soil was being brought down by the River Nile.

And they shall turn the rivers far away; and the brooks of defence shall be emptied and dried up: the reeds and flags shall wither [Isa. 19:6].

It is quite interesting that even today those "brooks," those outlets to the sea there at the delta, are filled up. It has been a wonderful place like the Garden of Eden, but it is not that now by any means. Those who have traveled to the land of Egypt are amazed to see that there is no great growth of vegetation along the banks of the Nile. There is no forest or heavy foliage such as is common along other great rivers.

Now notice what God says specifically:

The paper reeds by the brooks, by the mouth of the brooks, and every thing sown by the brooks, shall wither, be driven away, and be no more [Isa. 19:7].

The "paper reeds" are the papyri which were used in that day as paper is used today. It was one of the main industries of Egypt, and it added a great deal to the wealth of Egypt. After clay tablets, papyrus became the writing material of man. The Phoenicians introduced papyrus all over the civilized world of their day, and the main source of this writing material was raised along the Nile River. You won't find it there today. It no longer grows along the banks where it was indigenous. If you go there today, you will find papyri in front of the museum beside the pool that is there, and you see it growing at some of the wealthy homes, especially in the British colony at Cairo. It is a luxury; it is no longer the common plant which grew plentifully along the River Nile. God said it would cease. You can try to find a natural explanation for its dying out, but I believe that God had something to do with it.

> **The fishers also shall mourn, and all they that cast angle into the brooks shall lament, and they that spread nets upon the waters shall languish [Isa. 19:8].**

Fishing was another great industry in Egypt, as the Nile River abounded in fish. When the children of Israel came out of Egypt, they missed the fish they had eaten in Egypt. Of course, there were no fish in the desert. God gave them flesh to eat when He sent them quail; but, very frankly, they didn't care too much for quail on toast. They much preferred the fish in Egypt. The fish have disappeared, and to this day fishing is not one of the industries along the Nile. This prophecy was literally fulfilled. When I was in Egypt, I particularly watched for people fishing in the Nile. I don't think I saw over two or three people fishing! In Florida you see hundreds of people fishing along the canals, but you don't see fishing like that in Egypt. God said that the fishermen would mourn and lament—because they wouldn't catch anything.

> **Moreover they that work in fine flax, and they that weave networks, shall be confounded [Isa. 19:9].**

Egypt raised flax, and they wove it into remarkable linen. It even excelled the linen made in Ireland in our day. I have been told that while the Irish linen mills get about 180,000 feet of strands per pound, the Egyptian mills got 300,000—almost twice the amount. It was very much like silk. It is said that a fisherman could take a net made of that fine twined byssus linen and pull it through the ring on his hand! It

was this Egyptian linen that was used in Israel's wilderness tabernacle. The people had brought that wonderful linen with them.

Now God said that that industry would disappear, and it certainly
has disappeared. This prophecy has been literally fulfilled.

> **And they shall be broken in the purposes thereof, all
> that make sluices and ponds for fish [Isa. 19:10].**

The entire fishing industry was to disappear. This has been fulfilled
literally. Dr. F. C. Jennings writes, "Egypt's wealth, as already said,
practically consists in her river, because of its volume here called a
sea." All of that has disappeared.

> **Surely the princes of Zoan are fools, the counsel of the
> wise counsellors of Pharaoh is become brutish: how say
> ye unto Pharaoh, I am the son of the wise, the son of
> ancient kings? [Isa. 19:11].**

The royal line of the pharaohs intermarried so much—actually brother
married sister—that it produced offspring who were morons. God
said:

> **The princes of Zoan are become fools, the princes of
> Noph are deceived; they have also seduced Egypt, even
> they that are the stay of the tribes thereof [Isa. 19:13].**

"Noph" is Memphis as we know it.

"They have also seduced Egypt." We all know the sordid story of
Cleopatra (a Greek) who became queen of Egypt.

> **The Lord hath mingled a perverse spirit in the midst
> thereof: and they have caused Egypt to err in every work
> thereof, as a drunken man staggereth in his vomit [Isa.
> 19:14].**

This is a vivid picture of the reduction of Egypt to a base kingdom.

Neither shall there be any work for Egypt, which the head or tail, branch or rush, may do [Isa. 19:15].

According to this verse there would be the failure of industry and commerce. They would die, and poverty and wretchedness would overtake the nation. Isaiah has predicted that there will be failure of false religion, failure of material resources, and failure of spiritual power. When these disappeared, the prophecy that Egypt would become a base kingdom was fulfilled. All you have to do is to go to Cairo today to have this confirmed.

UNFULFILLED PROPHECY

In that day shall Egypt be like unto women: and it shall be afraid and fear because of the shaking of the hand of the LORD of hosts, which he shaketh over it [Isa. 19:16].

The phrase, "In that day," places this section in the future. "In that day" Egypt will be afraid like women; that will be their condition when they go into the Great Tribulation Period.

And the land of Judah shall be a terror unto Egypt, every one that maketh mention thereof shall be afraid in himself, because of the counsel of the LORD of hosts, which he hath determined against it [Isa. 19:17].

You may be thinking that this verse is being fulfilled in our day when we see buildings in Egypt, like the museum in Cairo, sandbagged and protected against a bomb attack.

In that day five cities in the land of Egypt speak the language of Canaan, and swear to the LORD of hosts; one shall be called, The city of destruction [Isa. 19:18].

This entire section looks toward the Day of the Lord for a complete fulfillment.

> In that day shall there be an altar to the LORD in the midst of the land of Egypt, and a pillar at the border thereof to the LORD.
>
> And it shall be for a sign and for a witness unto the LORD of hosts in the land of Egypt: for they shall cry unto the LORD because of the oppressors, and he shall send them a saviour, and a great one, and he shall deliver them [Isa. 19:19–20].

"An altar to the LORD" has been interpreted by some of the cults as the pyramid. The pyramid is neither an altar nor a pillar, but a monstrous mausoleum for the burying of kings and queens. What will be "a sign"? What will be an ensign? The cross will yet be the place to which Egypt will look instead of to a crescent.

> And the LORD shall be known to Egypt, and the Egyptians shall know the LORD in that day, and shall do sacrifice and oblation; yea, they shall vow a vow unto the LORD, and perform it.
>
> And the LORD shall smite Egypt: he shall smite and heal it: and they shall return even to the LORD, and he shall be entreated of them, and shall heal them [Isa. 19:21–22].

Egypt has a glorious future. The nation will enter and enjoy the kingdom with Israel. It may not look like this could be possible in the present hour. Only God can do this.

> In that day shall there be a highway out of Egypt to Assyria, and the Assyrian shall come into Egypt, and the Egyptian into Assyria, and the Egyptians shall serve with the Assyrians [Isa. 19:23].

This freeway will not be for soldiers and armies but for those going to Jerusalem to serve Christ the King.

> **In that day shall Israel be the third with Egypt and with Assyria, even a blessing in the midst of the land [Isa. 19:24].**

Note the exalted position of Egypt in the Kingdom.

> **Whom the LORD of hosts shall bless, saying, Blessed be Egypt my people, and Assyria the work of my hands, and Israel mine inheritance [Isa. 19:25].**

A blessing is yet to come to Egypt, a despised and debased nation.

The one great thought in chapter 20 is that in three years Israel would be invaded. Chapter 19 is closed on the high note of future blessing for Egypt in the millennial kingdom, and this chapter predicts coming events in the *near* future, which will prove the reliability of Isaiah as a prophet of God.

> **In the year that Tartan came unto Ashdod (when Sargon the king of Assyria sent him,) and fought against Ashdod, and took it [Isa. 20:1].**

Tartan was a general in the Assyrian army, mentioned in 2 Kings 18:17. Ashdod was a city in the northern kingdom of ten tribes. Sargon succeeded Shalmaneser (see 2 Kings 17:3).

This is the only place the name of Sargon is mentioned in the Bible. As recent as one hundred years ago historians maintained that Sargon never lived, because they could find no reference to him in secular history. However, archaeologists discovered that the Assyrian form of his name is Sharrukin. Abundant historical materials concerning his reign have come down to us.

> **At the same time spake the LORD by Isaiah the son of Amoz, saying, Go and loose the sackcloth from off thy**

loins, and put off thy shoe from thy foot. And he did so, walking naked and barefoot [Isa. 20:2].

Isaiah was to become a walking parable to Israel as a warning not to become confederate with Egypt. Probably Isaiah was not asked to go in the nude. Clothing was and is so essential to the customs of the East and nudity is so revolting that it is obvious that this was not intended. Isaiah was to lay aside his outward tunic of mourning. This would attract immediate and startling attention to the prophet. It would enable Isaiah to make his point publicly. It is well to note the words of F. Delitzsch at this point: "What Isaiah was therefore directed to do was simply opposed to common custom and not to moral decency."

And the LORD said, Like as my servant Isaiah hath walked naked and barefoot three years for a sign and wonder upon Egypt and upon Ethiopia [Isa. 20:3].

Isaiah was to walk through Israel to let them know what would happen to Egypt. As he walked, we are told, he would be for a sign and wonder for the people.

So shall the king of Assyria lead away the Egyptians prisoners, and the Ethiopians captives, young and old, naked and barefoot, even with their buttocks uncovered, to the shame of Egypt [Isa. 20:4].

Since Egypt could not protect herself (nor could Ethiopia), she would not be a reliable ally for Israel. Both Egypt and Ethiopia were invaded by Sargon of Assyria, and this shame which Isaiah had predicted came upon Egypt.

CHAPTER 21

THEME: Three burdens: Babylon *"desert of the sea,"* Edom *"Dumah,"* and Arabia

Isaiah is enumerating eleven "burdens," or judgments. In this chapter we are going to consider burdens seven, eight, and nine, which are against Babylon, Edom, and Arabia. These burdens are set forth by expressive symbols, and in the day they were given I am sure they were as clear to the people as the noonday sun. In fact, they were as clear to the people in Isaiah's day as the expressions "stars and stripes" and "Old Glory" are to every American. The insignia in this chapter are not quite so clear to us today, and as a result there has been some disagreement among Bible expositors about their meaning. They can be identified as Babylon, Edom, and Arabia, and each one will be considered separately as we go through this chapter. All were enemies or potential enemies of Israel. Each brought a particular misery upon God's people. Each has been judged in time.

This chapter is a neglected part of the Word of God. To prove this, let me ask you a question. When was the last time you heard a sermon or Bible study on this chapter of the Bible? I have a notion that you have never heard a study on Isaiah 21. This is another section of Scripture which confirms my position of a premillennial, pretribulation, dispensational interpretation of the Word of God. It is the only interpretation which would satisfy a passage like this, which is the reason all other systems stay clear of this chapter and other portions of God's Word with like teaching.

The remarkable thing in this chapter is that symbols are used. Now I believe in a *literal* interpretation of Scripture, but when symbolism is used, it always pictures *reality*. That is an important thing to remember. Many expositors call a teaching of Scripture symbolism in an attempt to make it disappear. Like a magician says, "hocus-pocus," and it's gone—so don't worry about it. My friend, let's not try to evaporate this section of Scripture, but let's study it to see what God is saying.

The burden of the desert of the sea. As whirlwinds in the south pass through; so it cometh from the desert, from a terrible land [Isa. 21:1].

"The desert of the sea" is a strange expression. It is like saying "the dryness of the water," or "how dry the water is." This may not be too peculiar to us since we have "dry ice" and "cold heat." Dr. F. C. Jennings translates this verse, "As sweep the whirlwinds through the south, so comes it from the desert, from the land that strikes with terror." This is a good interpretation of the verse, but it does not identify the nation. But if you keep reading, the nation is identified in verse 9: "Babylon is fallen, is fallen." So we know "the desert of the sea" is Babylon. Before Babylon became a world power, her doom was again predicted. We have already seen that. The first burden in chapters 13—14 was against Babylon. Babylon became so awe-inspiring and frightful, and represented so much in Scripture, that we have this further word concerning its doom. It was the first place of united rebellion against God at the tower of Babel, and it represents the last stronghold of rebellion against God. We find this in Revelation 17 and 18. Religious Babylon is presented in Revelation 17, and commercial Babylon is set forth in Revelation 18.

The expression, "desert of the sea," is a paradoxical phrase. Babylon was geographically located on a great desert plain beside the Euphrates River. It was irrigated by canals from the river. Jeremiah gives this description of Babylon, "O thou that dwellest upon many waters, abundant in treasures, thine end is come, and the measure of thy covetousness" (Jer. 51:13). The desert and the sea form a weird amalgamation here. This same fusion of desert and sea is made by John in Revelation. "So he carried me away in the spirit into the wilderness: and I saw a woman sit upon a scarlet coloured beast, full of names of blasphemy, having seven heads and ten horns" (Rev. 17:3). This is the desert where John beheld the mystery Babylon: ". . . Come hither; I will shew unto thee the judgment of the great whore that sitteth upon many waters" (Rev. 17:1). It was in the desert that John saw the "many waters." These two verses are symbolic, but they carry through the same pattern. We will find it again in Jerusalem.

Babylon, with its glitter and glamour and as the fountainhead of idolatry and false religion, was a mirage upon the desert. Isn't this tremendous!—"desert of the sea"—what a picture! Babylon was not a wonderful place. It was a mirage in the desert. It wasn't a spring or an oasis at all, but a place filled with idols and false religion. There was no life-giving water there for the souls of men. This is something that every pastor, every radio preacher, every church, and every church member ought to turn over in his mind. Is my church or am I a life-giving fountain, or am I just a mirage upon the desert of life?

A grievous vision is declared unto me; the treacherous dealer dealeth treacherously, and the spoiler spoileth. Go up, O Elam; besiege, O Media; all the sighing thereof have I made to cease [Isa. 21:2].

God commands the two-fold nation of Media-Persia to destroy and spoil the city. "Go up, O Elam [Persia]: besiege, O Media." That is exactly what happened. This is a prophecy that was given before the invasion took place.

Therefore are my loins filled with pain: pangs have taken hold upon me, as the pangs of a woman that travaileth: I was bowed down at the hearing of it; I was dismayed at the seeing of it.

My heart panted, fearfulness afrighted me: the night of my pleasure hath he turned into fear unto me [Isa. 21:3-4].

Once again Isaiah is moved with great feeling and emotion when he learns of the coming devastation. This is the heart of God revealed, desiring to show mercy and loath to judge even so frightful a foe. God's love is as evident here as in the tears of Jeremiah. No one can rejoice in the judgment of God. God says that His judgment is His "strange" work. He does not want to judge you; He wants to save you, but the choice is yours. He doesn't want to judge nations either, and that choice is up to them.

Prepare the table, watch in the watchtower, eat, drink: arise, ye princes, and anoint the shield [Isa. 21:5].

This verse reads as if it were an eyewitness account of the destruction of Babylon as recorded by Daniel (see Dan. 5). Remember, this was recorded about two hundred years before it transpired. In the midst of the banquet of Belshazzar, the Median general, Gobryas, detoured the river that flowed through the city and marched his army on the dry river bed underneath the walls of the city. He took the city by surprise and shock. This is something that God said would take place.

And he cried, A lion: My Lord, I stand continually upon the watchtower in the daytime, and I am set in my ward whole nights:

And behold, here cometh a chariot of men, with a couple of horsemen. And he answered and said, Babylon is fallen, is fallen; and all the graven images of her gods he hath broken unto the ground [Isa. 21:8-9].

The watchman on the walls of the city tells the people inside what he sees. He says, "As I look out on the desert, here comes a chariot of men, with a couple of horses." They are messengers, and their message is "Babylon is fallen, is fallen." The watchman brings word to the king of Babylon that it has fallen (see Jer. 51:31-33). All of Babylon's graven images of her gods are broken unto the ground. This is a sigh of sorrow as well as relief. Babylon was the source of all idolatry.

O my threshing, and the corn of my floor: that which I have heard of the LORD of hosts, the God of Israel, have I declared unto you [Isa. 21:10].

Harvest is the time of judgment. In John 4:35 our Lord said, "Say not ye, There are yet four months, and then cometh harvest? behold, I say unto you, Lift up your eyes, and look on the fields; for they are white already to harvest." Our Lord said this at the end of the age of law, when judgment was coming against Israel who had had the Law for almost fifteen hundred years. Harvest is the time of judgment.

There is a book I would like to recommend to you at this point, because we are going to study more about Babylon in the Books of Jeremiah, Ezekiel, and Daniel. Hislop's book, *The Two Babylons*, would be a valuable addition to your library.

BURDEN OF EDOM

The burden of Dumah. He calleth to me out of Seir, Watchman, what of the night? Watchman, what of the night? [Isa. 21:11].

Who is "Dumah"? Dumah is a symbolic word. Isaiah played upon words to bring out a deeper meaning. We have already seen that. He used words to carry a message to the people. "Dumah" is Edom with the *E* removed. You take the *E* off Edom, and you have *Dumah* which means "silence." Our word *dumb* is closer to the intent and purpose of Isaiah. Edom is still a land of deathlike silence.

Seir means "rough or hairy." Esau was the first Seir man (see Gen. 25:25). He was hairy, and he dwelt in Mount Seir (see Gen. 36:8). *Seir* also means "storms." It was a land swept with storms. "Silence and Storm." What a play on words, and what a message!

Edom is obviously the country involved. Out of the land of silence and storm comes this inquiry, which is twice repeated: "Watchman, what of the night?" In other words, "How much of the night is gone?" How long will it be before God's glory will be revealed when the ". . . Sun of righteousness [shall] arise with healing in his wings . . ." (Mal. 4:2)?

The watchman said, The morning cometh, and also the night: if ye will inquire, inquire ye: return, come [Isa. 21:12].

You see, both morning and night are coming. What will be glory for some will be doom for others. What will be light for God's people will be night for Edomites, the men of the flesh who have rejected God.

BURDEN OF ARABIA

The burden upon Arabia. In the forest in Arabia shall ye lodge, O ye travelling companies of Dedanim [Isa. 21:13].

"Arabia" seems clear enough, but again this is a word with a double meaning. It can be made to mean *evening* by changing the vowel points. The Hebrew language is a language of consonants with no vowels. Instead it had vowel points, which are little marks above the consonants. Scholars have added vowels to the Hebrew words to make them more readable. In this verse the meaning is quite obvious: it was evening in the history of Arabia. It was later than they thought. Arabia was the land of the Ishmeelites, the Bedouin tribes of the desert—the modern Arabs. It is interesting that God speaks of them. Abraham's sons, Ishmael and Isaac, never did get along. Their descendants don't get along today either. The Arabs and the Jews are still at each other's throats. If Abraham could see what is going on now, I wonder if he would think the sin he committed was a small sin. My friend, sin never ceases working itself out in the human story.

The inhabitants of the land of Tema brought water to him that was thirsty, they prevented with their bread him that fled.

For they fled from the swords, from the drawn sword, and from the bent bow, and from the grievousness of war.

For thus hath the Lord said unto me, Within a year, according to the years of an hireling, and all the glory of Kedar shall fail [Isa. 21:14–16].

There was a coming judgment upon this land and its people. This chapter of poetic beauty and heart sorrow should not end on this note. It may be "evening" here, but God's day is reckoned "the evening and

the morning"—". . . the evening and the morning were the first day"
(Gen. 1:5).

The morning is coming; the night of weeping will soon be over,
and the new day will dawn. Man's evening of failure, sin, and darkness will end, and God's morning will be ushered in by the coming of
the Sun of Righteousness.

CHAPTER 22

*THEME: The burden of the valley of vision (Jerusalem);
the history of Shebna and Eliakim*

This burden evidently refers to Jerusalem, as we shall point out under the comments on the verses. The burdens began way off at a distance in Babylon, and they have continued to come nearer to Jerusalem. Now the storm breaks in all of its fury upon the Holy City.

BURDEN OF JERUSALEM

The burden of the valley of vision. What aileth thee now, that thou art wholly gone up to the housetops? [Isa. 22:1].

The "valley of vision" refers to Jerusalem, as verses 4, 8, 9, and 10 imply. The expression, "valley of vision," is another of Isaiah's paradoxical statements. *Mountain* of vision would be understood, because the mountain is the place of the far view. Moses stood on Mount Nebo to view the land of promise. Our Lord looked over Jerusalem from the Mount of Olives. But in Scripture a valley symbolizes a place of sorrow, humbleness, and death. Because the vision here is one of sorrow and coming battle, the valley is the proper place for this vision.

Curiosity and fear send people to the housetop to inquire about the approaching danger. See the Assyrian siege of Jerusalem in Isaiah 36 and 37. In the last siege our Lord warns these people to leave the housetops and flee (see Matt. 24:16–17).

Therefore said I, Look away from me: I will weep bitterly, labour not to comfort me, because of the spoiling of the daughter of my people [Isa. 22:4].

"My people" are, of course, the people of Israel.

> Ye have seen also the breaches of the city of David, that they are many: and ye gathered together the waters of the lower pool.
>
> And ye have numbered the houses of Jerusalem, and the houses have ye broken down to fortify the wall [Isa. 22:9-10].

Hezekiah actually took these precautions in defending Jerusalem (see 2 Chron. 32). One of the things he did was to put a wall around the fountain so that the city would not run out of water. You can still see it in the land today.

This section refers to the future. As Dr. F. C. Jennings puts it, "The history eventuated in the deliverance of Jerusalem, the prophecy in its capture; therefore the history does not fulfill it."

Just what siege and enemy is in the mind of the prophet? Persia is mentioned by name, but Jerusalem was in ruins while Persia was in power. Apparently all the enemies who have come up against Jerusalem are before us here, from the Assyrians who only laid a siege but did not enter the city, to the last enemy from the north who will threaten the city but will not enter. The interval between these two has seen this city captured more than any other. This is the burden of Jerusalem.

BRIEF FROM THE CASE OF SHEBNA AND ELIAKIM

The unusual insertion at this point of an historical document out of the archives of Jerusalem during the reign of Hezekiah is worth noting.

Many have seen a picture of the Antichrist in Shebna, while Eliakim sets before us none other than the Lord Jesus Christ who will supplant the Antichrist in this world

> Thus saith the Lord GOD of hosts, Go, get thee unto this treasurer, even unto Shebna, which is over the house, and say [Isa. 22:15].

Shebna was secretary of the treasury, a cheap politician under Heze-kiah. Apparently he was misappropriating funds (see 2 Kings 18:18; 19:2; Isa. 36:3;37:2).

> **What hast thou here? and whom hast thou here, that thou hast hewed thee out a sepulchre here, as he that heweth him out a sepulchre on high, and that graveth an habitation for himself in a rock? [Isa. 22:16].**

Shebna was building a tomb to perpetuate his name. It was ironical, as he was to die and be buried in a foreign land (vv. 17–18).

> **And I will drive thee from thy station, and from thy state shall he pull thee down [Isa. 22:19].**

Shebna, I think is just an adumbration of Antichrist.

> **And it shall come to pass in that day, that I will call my servant Eliakim the son of Hilkiah:**

> **And I will clothe him with thy robe, and strengthen him with thy girdle, and I will commit thy government into his hand: and he shall be a father to the inhabitants of Jerusalem, and to the house of Judah [Isa. 22:20–21].**

Eliakim was the statesman who succeeded Shebna. Eliakim was an unselfish man. He and Shebna are in contrast here. Isaiah has brought together these men who are more than paradoxes—they are opposites. Shebna pictures the Antichrist, and Eliakim pictures Christ. The language is typical.

> **And the key of the house of David will I lay upon his shoulder; so he shall open, and none shall shut; and he shall shut, and none shall open [Isa. 22:22].**

This verse reminds us of the words of Christ in the New Testament: "And to the angel of the church in Philadelphia write; These things saith he that is holy, he that is true, he that hath the key of David, he that openeth, and no man shutteth; and shutteth, and no man openeth" (Rev. 3:7). How wonderful it is, my friend, to place our lives in the hands of Him who is able to close or open any door!

> **And I will fasten him as a nail in a sure place; and he shall be for a glorious throne to his father's house.**

> **And they shall hang upon him all the glory of his father's house, the offspring and the issue, all vessels of small quantity, from the vessels of cups, even to all the vessels of flagons [Isa. 22:23–24].**

Our salvation likewise hangs on Him.

> **In that day, saith the LORD of hosts, shall the nail that is fastened in the sure place be removed, and be cut down, and fall; and the burden that was upon it shall be cut off: for the LORD hath spoken it [Isa. 22:25].**

"In that day" refers to the Great Tribulation Period, as we have seen, and this verse refers to Shebna as he pictures the Antichrist. A great many people will put their trust in the Antichrist who is to come. They will look to him for help. They will think he is Christ, but he will be just a nail that will fall.

My friend, have you ever had that experience? You drive a good nail into the wall, hang a heavy coat on it, and it comes down. The Lord Jesus Christ is the nail in a sure place. Shebna was a nail that came down, and so will all others who are like him. Are you hanging everything you've got on the nail that is in a sure place? Many people are not. They are hanging everything they have on something that is not sure. For instance, they make investments. A man told me, "I trusted a lawyer, and he made a mistake." He wasn't a nail in a sure place. Some folk have even trusted a preacher and have found that he was not a nail in a sure place. Only Christ is a nail in a sure place. I hope you are hanging your life and everything you have on Him.

CHAPTER 23

THEME: The burden of Tyre

In this chapter we come to the eleventh and last burden against the nations. A burden, as we have seen, is a judgment, and these judgments were leveled against the nations around Israel. Each one of these great nations represents or sets before us some principle, philosophy, or system which God must judge. Let me give a recapitulation of these eleven nations and what they represent.

1. *Babylon* represents false religions and idolatry. Idolatry in our land is covetousness, which is the overwhelming desire to have more and to give ourselves to the accumulation of the material things of the world.

2. *Palestine* represents true religion which has become apostate. Today you find that the same thing has happened in many churches. They go through rituals, they even repeat the Apostles' Creed and the Lord's Prayer. From all outward appearances they seem to be resting upon the Bible, but in reality they deny everything that is in it. They are apostate, which means they are standing away from what they once believed.

3. *Moab* represents formal religion; that is, having a form of godliness, but denying the power thereof.

Many of us today could be identified with one of these three. Some of us are giving our lives to the accumulation of material things, and our eyes are filled with the things we want. We are covetous.

Some of us have been brought up in Bible-believing churches but have turned away from their teachings. Others of us go to church and follow forms, ceremonies, and rituals, which are beautiful but dead as a dodo bird.

4. *Damascus* represents compromise. That is the position that most churches (even fundamental churches) are in today. Thank God for those churches that are standing true!

5. *Ethiopia* represents missions. How we need to be involved in getting out the Word of God!

6. *Egypt* represents the world. Israel was told to stay out of Egypt—that is where Abraham got into trouble. And we are admonished, "Love not the world." Many of us are having trouble with the world.

7. *Persia* (Babylon) represents luxury. My, how most of us love luxury in our affluent society.

8. *Edom* represents the flesh. Many people serve the flesh today.

9. *Arabia* represents war. These are two groups of people in our contemporary society: the hawks and the doves. Both are of the world, and the only difference I see in them is that the peace group tells us they are for peace, but they are willing to *fight* for it!

10. *Valley of vision,* which is Jerusalem, represents not religion but politics. Some think that in politics will be found the solutions to the problems of the world.

11. *Tyre* represents commercialism (big business). I would say that the great sin of America today is commercialism, believing that the almighty dollar can solve all our problems. When a problem comes up, Congress votes for a little money, and people for whom it is intended never get it, of course. Every poverty program has hurt rather than helped the poor. Why? Because godless men just don't have the right solutions. The poor haven't learned that yet, because they are also far from God. It is only the Lord Jesus Christ who has any love for the poor and really knows how to help them.

Now let us look at the burden of Tyre. Tyre and Sidon were the two great cities of the Phoenicians. Sidon was the mother city, and she was soon surpassed by her proud and rich daughter, Tyre.

The ships of the Phoenicians entered all ports of the Mediterranean Sea and even penetrated the uncharted ocean beyond the Pillars of Hercules. The vessels of Phoenicia brought tin from Great Britain—in fact, the meaning of *Brittania* is "the land of tin." The Phoenicians were aggresssive and progressive people. Carthage, in North Africa, was settled by them. Carthage, the great enemy of Rome, was a Phoenician city, and Cyprus owed its prosperity to trading with Tyre. There were also other centers that the Phoenicians founded—Tarshish for instance. You remember that when Jonah tried to flee from the Lord, he bought a ticket for Tarshish. Tarshish was on the southern coast of Spain. Who founded it? The Phoenicians did. It is also of interest that the Phoenicians invented the alphabet.

Hiram, king of Tyre, was one of the great friends of King David. When we get to Ezekiel 26, we are going to see a remarkable prophecy concerning Tyre, which had an exact fulfillment. God said that Tyre would be destroyed by Babylon and would be taken into captivity for seventy years just as Judah went into captivity for seventy years. The people of Tyre returned to their land, as did Israel, after the captivity and rebuilt their city on an island in the Mediterranean Sea about half a mile from the old city. God said that the ruins of the old city would be scraped (see Ezek. 26:4), and, later, Alexander the Great scraped the ancient site of Tyre to make a causeway to the island city. He was wise enough not to attempt a battle by sea, because the Phoenicians were experts with ships; so he built a causeway from the old city on the mainland to the new city on the island. I've walked down that causeway and it is filled with broken pieces of pottery. I could have filled tubs with pieces of pottery, but, of course, no one is allowed to do that. I put one little piece in my pocket, because it looked as if there was plenty to spare. Where did all the pottery and pillars and rubble come from? It came from the ruins of ancient Tyre. Alexander the Great literally scraped the surface of the old city to build his causeway, and you cannot tell where the site of the old Tyre used to be—it's all out there in the causeway. When Alexander took the city, the prophecy of Ezekiel was fulfilled exactly as God said it would be: "And I will make thee like the top of a rock: thou shalt be a place to spread nets upon; thou shalt be built no more: for I the LORD have spoken it, saith the Lord GOD" (Ezek. 26:14). My friend, today there is a little Turkish town near there, but the site of ancient Tyre is still in ruins.

If an atheist wants to disprove the Word of God, I suggest that he do more than stand on a street corner and blab about the fact that he doesn't believe in God. I challenge him to go over to the ancient site of Tyre and rebuild the city. However, I warn him that others have tried to do it and have failed.

In fact, there is a ready-made city, the rock-hewn city of Petra, that is all ready to be moved into. The only problem is that God said it would not be inhabited. Anyone can try to start a colony there, but he won't succeed. A German unbeliever took a group of people to Petra and tried to start a colony, but it didn't last long. You won't succeed either, friend. God said that Tyre won't be rebuilt and that Petra won't be inhabited.

DIVINE RESPONSIBILITY FOR TYRE'S DESTRUCTION

The burden of Tyre. Howl, ye ships of Tarshish; for it is laid waste, so that there is no house, no entering in: from the land of Chittim it is revealed to them [Isa. 23:1].

The picture here is that of ships coming home to Tyre from Tarshish where there is a colony of the Phoenicians. Word is brought to them that Tyre has been destroyed. As they sail near, they see the smoke of the city. Then they see that the city has been leveled and the harbor blocked. It will no longer be a great commercial center.

Be still, ye inhabitants of the isle; thou whom the merchants of Zidon, that pass over the sea, have replenished [Isa. 23:2].

"Zidon," or Sidon, was about thirty miles up the coast from Tyre. Tyre and Sidon go together like pork and beans go together. They were the two leading cities of the Phoenicians. The prominent sea merchants of Sidon had made Tyre the great city it was. It is interesting that the prophecy concerning the destruction of Tyre was literally fulfilled. But destruction was not predicted for Sidon, and Sidon continues as a city today. Currently, Sidon is the place to which oil is brought to be loaded on shipboard and taken to other parts of the world.

> And by great waters the seed of Sihor, the harvest of the
> river, is her revenue; and she is a mart of nations [Isa.
> 23:3].

Sihor means "black" and refers to the Upper Nile, the silt of which
flooded Egypt and made it fertile. The wealth of Egypt had flowed
through the port of Tyre, and now that is ended, and there is going to
be a depression—a real one!

> Be thou ashamed, O Zidon: for the sea hath spoken,
> even the strength of the sea, saying, I travail not, nor
> bring forth children, neither do I nourish up young
> men, nor bring up virgins [Isa. 23:4].

There is a suggestion here that Tyre is the daughter of Sidon. Histori-
cally this is accurate.

> As at the report concerning Egypt, so shall they be
> sorely pained at the report of Tyre [Isa. 23:5].

The destruction of Tyre ruined the commerce of Egypt in that day.

> Pass ye over to Tarshish; howl, ye inhabitants of the isle
> [Isa. 23:6].

The fall of Tyre caused universal mourning, even to a colony that was
way over on the southern coast of Spain. Some of the inhabitants of
Tyre escaped in ships to Tarshish, when Nebuchadnezzar destroyed
the city.

> Is this your joyous city, whose antiquity is of ancient
> days? her own feet shall carry her afar off to sojourn
> [Isa. 23:7].

Any great commercial center is a city which is also a fun center because there will be many things in that city that are pleasing to the

flesh. Now the Tyrians are urged to flee as far as possible because this city which was formerly a "joyous city" has come to an end.

> **Who hath taken this counsel against Tyre, the crowning city, whose merchants are princes, whose traffickers are the honourable of the earth? [Isa. 23:8].**

"The crowning city" means the *giver of crowns*. You see, Tyre established crown colonies. Great Britain has done the same thing in more recent times. A crown colony is under the legislation and administration of the crown rather than having its own constitution and representative government.

> **The Lord of hosts hath purposed it, to stain the pride of all glory, and to bring into contempt all the honourable of the earth [Isa. 23:9].**

It was the Lord of hosts who had determined the destruction of Tyre. He offers no apologies for making the arrangement.

HUMAN RESPONSIBILITY FOR TYRE'S DESTRUCTION

> **Pass through thy land as a river, O daughter of Tarshish: there is no more strength [Isa. 23:10].**

The "river" is the Nile. As the Nile has overflowed her banks, the colony of Tarshish is now free to do as she pleases since Tyre has fallen and is no longer able to control her.

"There is no more strength" means that there is no girdle that holds her up or binds her.

> **He stretched out his hand over the sea, he shook the kingdoms: the Lord hath given a commandment against the merchant city, to destroy the strong holds thereof [Isa. 23:11].**

Have you noticed this threefold description of Tyre? In verse 7 Tyre is called a "joyous city." In verse 8 Tyre is called a "crowning city." In verse 11 Tyre is called a "merchant city." All three of these are apt descriptions of Tyre.

And he said, Thou shalt no more rejoice, O thou oppressed virgin, daughter of Zidon: arise pass over to Chittim; there also shalt thou have no rest [Isa. 23:12].

What is suggested in verse 4 is plainly declared here. Tyre is the daughter of Sidon. Sidon was the older city, and rich merchants from there had founded Tyre and given her prestige. The joy of prosperity was to disappear. Both Tyre and Sidon would suffer.

"Pass over to Chittim"—probably some thought that by fleeing to Cyprus they might make a fresh beginning. In this, too, they were to be disappointed. God was responsible for what happened to them, although He used human instruments.

Behold the land of the Chaldeans; this people was not, till the Assyrian founded it for them that dwell in the wilderness: they set up the towers thereof, they raised up the palaces thereof; and he brought it to ruin [Isa. 23:13].

When Assyria was a great nation, Chaldea (Babylon) was just a hick town. Now Babylon is the ruler of the world.

Howl, ye ships of Tarshish: for your strength is laid waste [Isa. 23:14].

RECOVERY OF TYRE—PARTIAL AND COMPLETE

And it shall come to pass in that day, that Tyre shall be forgotten seventy years, according to the days of one king: after the end of seventy years shall Tyre sing as an harlot [Isa. 23:15].

Tyre was to go into captivity for seventy years.

> **And it shall come to pass after the end of seventy years,
> that the LORD will visit Tyre, and she shall turn to her
> hire, and shall commit fornication with all the king-
> doms of the world upon the face of the earth [Isa. 23:17].**

At the end of seventy years Tyre was to return and begin once again her world commerce. Once more she would become a great commercial center, and she would commit fornication with all the kingdoms of the world upon the face of the earth. The prophet compares Tyre to a harlot plying her unholy trade. That is the way God speaks of these great commercial centers.

Now we move down the ages to the last days, the time of the Great Tribulation. Here we find that Tyre will again be a great nation and will enter the Millennium.

> **And her merchandise and her hire shall be holiness to
> the LORD: it shall not be treasured nor laid up; for her
> merchandise shall be for them that dwell before the
> LORD, to eat sufficiently, and for durable clothing [Isa.
> 23:18].**

"Her merchandise shall be for them that dwell before the LORD." Now it is all dedicated to the Lord. "And the daughter of Tyre shall be there with a gift; even the rich among the people shall entreat thy favour" (Ps. 45:12).

CHAPTER 24

THEME: Coming—the Great Tribulation

This brings us to a new section, although the theme is still judgment. Chapter 23 concluded the judgment against the nations. We have seen God's judgment against the nations. We have seen God's judgment snowballing from nation to nation, and now it comes down to the final judgment that is coming upon the earth, which our Lord Jesus Christ labeled the Great Tribulation Period. Both F. Delitzsch and F. C. Jennings consider this section thoroughly eschatological; that is, it refers to the final judgment from God which will come upon the whole world. In contrast to the judgments upon the nations in chapters 13—23 which have largely been fulfilled, this final judgment is entirely future.

WORLDWIDE JUDGMENT FROM GOD

Behold the Lord maketh the earth empty, and maketh it waste, and turneth it upside down, and scattereth abroad the inhabitants thereof [Isa. 24:1].

"Earth" in this verse is the Hebrew word *erets* and could mean either the land of Israel or the whole world. The whole world conforms better to the context in this chapter. Actually, the judgment could be said to be twofold, referring not only to the land of Israel, but to the entire world.

Therefore hath the curse devoured the earth, and they that dwell therein are desolate: therefore the inhabitants of the earth are burned, and few men left [Isa. 24:6].

God promised Noah that He would never destroy the earth again with a flood. Note here that the judgment is fire—"burned." Second Peter

3:6–7 says, "Whereby the world that then was, being overflowed with water, perished: But the heavens and the earth, which are now, by the same word are kept in store, reserved unto fire against the day of judgment and perdition of ungodly men."

PRESERVATION OF THE SAINTS

In verses 13–15 we see that the saints are preserved through the Great Tribulation Period.

> When thus it shall be in the midst of the land among the people, there shall be as the shaking of an olive tree, and as the gleaning grapes when the vintage is done.
>
> They shall lift up their voice, they shall sing for the majesty of the LORD, they shall cry aloud from the sea.
>
> Wherefore glorify ye the LORD in the fires, even the name of the LORD God of Israel in the isles of the sea [Isa. 24:13–15].

The remnant will be small, and they will lift up their voices to glorify God. Now in the time of testing, during the Tribulation, they will be able to glorify the Lord, "even the name of the LORD God of Israel." So there is to be a remnant at that time, which will be of Israel, and also out to the very "isles of the sea," which will include the whole earth, of course.

UNIVERSAL AND UNPARALLELED SUFFERING

> From the uttermost part of the earth have we heard songs, even glory to the righteous. But I said, My leanness, my leanness, woe unto me! the treacherous dealers have dealt treacherously; yea, the treacherous dealers have dealt very treacherously [Isa. 24:16].

"My leanness, my leanness"—when the prophet sees the awful character of the destruction of the Great Tribulation, he cries out, as Dr.

Jennings translates it, "My misery, my misery." It is going to be a terrible time.

Our Lord described this period of time in just as striking language when He said, "For then shall be great tribulation such as was not since the beginning of the world to this time, no, nor ever shall be. And except those days should be shortened, there should no flesh be saved: but for the elect's sake those days shall be shortened" (Matt. 24:21–22).

Fear, and the pit, and the snare, are upon thee, O inhabitant of the earth [Isa. 24:17].

This verse states that there are three dangers that will be upon the inhabitants of the earth in that day.

1. "Fear"—there is no freedom from fear here. From the time of the Atlantic Truce, drawn up by Winston Churchill and Franklin Roosevelt, politicians have talked about bringing freedom from fear to the world. How about it? Is the world free from fear today? Mobs are marching. Dissatisfaction and fear are everywhere. And fear will be multiplied during the Tribulation.

2. "Pit"—is danger of death. Hanging over the world today is the threat of the atom bomb, and it spells frightful death to the population of the world. God says He won't let the population be destroyed. The Lord Jesus said, "Except those days be shortened, no flesh would be able to survive," but He is going to shorten those days.

3. "Snare"—is deception. What the Lord Jesus Christ said as He began the Olivet discourse fits right into the Great Tribulation Period. In Matthew 24:4 the Lord said, ". . . Take heed that no man deceive you." It will be a time when people will believe that they are entering into the Millennium. We get the impression today that some of the great world leaders think they are going to bring in the Millennium. Well, they are going to bring in nothing but the Great Tribulation Period, and the Antichrist will take over. The world will think they are entering the Millennium, when in fact they are entering the Tribulation. One of the things that will characterize the Antichrist is deception. He will be a deceiver. After all, that is what his papa, the Devil is.

How many people there are who are being deceived today! They are deceived about life. How many people are even thinking about eternity? Not many. Most people think only of the here and now. Science is now rejecting the creation account—they don't want it. This is a great day of deception. You can be deceived by science; you can be deceived by politicians; you can be deceived by the news media; you can be deceived by the military; and you can be deceived by all of the malcontents who are protesting today. The only help available is the Lord Jesus Christ. Turn to Him. He has been made unto us wisdom, and He is the only hope. During the Tribulation people will be deceived; the Antichrist will be able to look at the world and privately say, "Suckers!" And that's what they will be. The Devil has said that about the human race for a long time, and that is what we are unless we turn to Christ.

> **And it shall come to pass, that he who fleeth from the noise of the fear shall fall into the pit; and he that cometh up out of the midst of the pit shall be taken in the snare: for the windows from on high are open, and the foundations of the earth do shake [Isa. 24:18].**

Those who don't go down into the pit of death will be snared. The Book of Revelation says that one fourth of the population is going to be taken out at one time in a great judgment, and at another time one third of the population will die.

TRIBULATION SAINTS ARE RAISED
FROM THE DEAD

This is a marvelous passage of Scripture that speaks of resurrection.

> **And they shall be gathered together, as prisoners are gathered in the pit, and shall be shut up in the prison, and after many days shall they be visited [Isa. 24:22].**

They shall go down into death; then they will be raised from the dead. I believe the meaning of this is that the Tribulation saints will have part in the first resurrection. They will be raised from the dead (see Rev. 20:4).

The Great Tribulation will end with the coming of the King (see Rev. 19:11–16).

> **Then the moon shall be confounded, and the sun ashamed, when the LORD of hosts shall reign in mount Zion, and in Jerusalem, and before his ancients gloriously [Isa. 24:23].**

"The moon shall be confounded, and the sun ashamed"—even nature is going to respond to the King when He comes to rule. Christ Jesus is the only One who can end this period known as the Great Tribulation.

CHAPTERS 25—27

THEME: Coming—the kingdom

After the Lord Jesus comes and ends the Tribulation, He establishes the kingdom. Chapters 25 and 26 bring us into the kingdom age. The King is coming, and there will be the kingdom of heaven upon this earth. This has been predicted throughout the Old Testament. And when John the Baptist began his ministry, his message was, ". . . Repent ye: for the kingdom of heaven is at hand" (Matt. 3:2). Then the Lord Jesus took up the theme, ". . . the kingdom of heaven is at hand" (Matt. 4:17).

But He was rejected as King. You can't have a kingdom without a king. When He was rejected as King, He could then say to individuals, "Come unto me, all ye that labour and are heavy laden, and I will give you rest" (Matt. 11:28). This is still His invitation today. It is a message to be sent out to individuals in our day asking them to exercise their free wills. Whether you know it or not, you are making a decision today. You are either accepting Him or rejecting Him. There is no neutral ground. Our Lord said, "He that is not with me is against me . . ." (Matt. 12:30).

This wonderful twenty-fifth chapter is a song, a song of three stanzas. This chapter, like chapter 12, is a paean of praise, a song of undiluted joy.

PRAISE TO GOD FOR DELIVERANCE
FROM ALL ENEMIES

O Lord, thou art my God; I will exalt thee, I will praise thy name; for thou hast done wonderful things; thy counsels of old are faithfulness and truth [Isa. 25:1].

This is praise to God for deliverance. This is a song of sheer delight, wonder, and worship. This comes from a heart full to overflowing, for the worshipper has come into a new knowledge of who God is and what He has done.

This is not the average song service that you have in church on Wednesday night. Some of the saints sit there and wonder why they came in the first place. Those who are singing this song are those who are eager to worship God because of His faithfulness and because He is true. These are the attributes of Deity, and they are foreign to humanity. The psalmist says, "It is better to trust in the LORD than to put confidence in man" (Ps. 118:8). Faithfulness is the fruit of the Spirit, not the work of the flesh. Truth is the very opposite of man. In Psalm 116:11 David said, "I said in my *haste*, All men are liars" (italics mine). I remember Dr. W. I. Carroll commenting, "I have had a lot of time to think it over, and I still agree with David."

> **For thou hast made of a city an heap; of a defenced city a ruin: a palace of strangers to be no city; it shall never be built [Isa. 25:2].**

All of the past is gone now. They are delivered from the enemies of the past. They no longer need a wall around a city to protect them.

> **Therefore shall the strong people glorify thee, the city of the terrible nations shall fear thee [Isa. 25:3].**

Does this mean worldwide conversion? I believe it does, for this is the Millennium. Man will turn to God in that day. The greatest turning to God is in the future when the night of sin and Great Tribulation will be past. Weeping shall endure for a night, but joy cometh in the morning. That is what we have here. There will be boundless joy during the kingdom age.

> **Thou shalt bring down the noise of strangers, as the heat in a dry place; even the heat with the shadow of a cloud: the branch of the terrible ones shall be brought low [Isa. 25:5].**

They recall the awful blasphemy of the last days personified in one of whom it is written: "Who opposeth and exalteth himself above all that is called God, or that is worshipped; so that he as God sitteth in the temple of God, shewing himself that he is God" (2 Thess. 2:4). The Antichrist will be put down as are all the enemies of God.

PRAISE TO GOD FOR PROVISION
OF PRESENT NEEDS

And in this mountain shall the LORD of hosts make unto all people a feast of fat things, a feast of wines on the lees, of fat things full of marrow, of wines on the lees well refined [Isa. 25:6].

"Fat things" have to do with physical provision certainly. The redeemed earth will produce bountifully. (Eating fat things in that day will not be a problem—you won't have to worry about putting on weight!) However, the "fat things" are likewise the wonderful spiritual feast in that day. I think there will be Bible classes held during the Millennium. I don't know, but maybe the Lord will let me teach one of them.

He will swallow up death in victory; and the Lord GOD will wipe away tears from off all faces; and the rebuke of his people shall he take away from off all the earth: for the LORD hath spoken it [Isa. 25:8].

This verse is quoted by Paul in 1 Corinthians 15:54, which says, "So when this corruptible shall have put on incorruption, and this mortal shall have put on immortality, then shall be brought to pass the saying that is written, Death is swallowed up in victory."

PRAISE TO GOD IN ANTICIPATION
OF FUTURE JOYS

And it shall be said in that day, Lo, this is our God; we have waited for him, and he will save us: this is the

LORD; we have waited for him, we will be glad and rejoice in his salvation [Isa. 25:9].

As we come to the final stanza, attention is drawn to the person of
God. It is with Him that men have to do. The world will be deceived by
Antichrist, but the real Christ, the real Messiah, the real Ruler of this
earth will come. His salvation is going to be vital to man in that day.
Man "will be glad and rejoice in his salvation."

Now this is a strange verse:

For in this mountain shall the hand of the LORD rest, and
Moab shall be trodden down under him, even as straw is
trodden down for the dunghill [Isa. 25:10].

Why is Moab introduced here? I will be very frank with you; it is difficult to say. When Moab is up, God is down. When God is up, Moab is
down. In the kingdom Moab is down, and God will be on top. As you
may remember, Moab represents a form of godliness but denies the
power thereof.

And the fortress of the high fort of thy walls shall he
bring down, lay low, and bring to the ground, even to the
dust [Isa. 25:12].

All the pride of man will be brought down. This is the period when
the meek shall inherit the earth (Matt. 5:5). The meek are not doing
too well in our day!

Chapter 26 continues the kingdom theme.

THE KINGDOM

In that day shall this song be sung in the land of Judah;
We have a strong city; salvation will God appoint for
walls and bulwarks [Isa. 26:1].

This is their prospect. In that day this song will be sung in Judah.
They don't have this song today, friend. It is obvious that the present
return to Israel is not a fulfillment of prophecy.

> **With my soul have I desired thee in the night; yea, with
> my spirit within me will I seek thee early: for when thy
> judgments are in the earth, the inhabitants of the world
> will learn righteousness [Isa. 26:9].**

"With my soul have I *desired* thee in the night." I wonder if you and I
recognize the great need for communion with Christ. In the little book
of the Song of Solomon, the bride said, "Let him kiss me with the
kisses of his mouth . . ." (Song 1:2). That was the kiss of pardon and of
peace and of passion. Then the bride, recognizing that she can't rise to
the heights she desires, says, "Draw me, we will run after thee . . ."
(Song 1:4). Isaiah is expressing the same thought here. "With my soul
have I *desired* thee in the night." My friend, do we have that passion
for God? I hear a lot of pseudo-love today, and a smattering of spiritual-
ity. I see people pretending to be pious and hear them quoting plati-
tudes. I get tired of hearing, "Oh, I love the Lord, and I want to serve
Him." My friend, when you lie on your bed at night, do you have a
desire for God? Do you really want Him? Do you have a real passion for
Him? Are you able to say, "Draw me, and I will run after thee."

In the time of the Millennium they will be saying, "With my soul
have I desired thee in the night; yea; with my spirit within me will I
seek thee early."

I confess that many times I find myself running from Him. I find
myself running ahead of Him, out of His will, and then the tensions
come. I am frustrated, and I say, "O, I've left Him. I've gotten away
from Him. I am not close to Him." I don't see many people crying out
for God today. I don't mean to be critical, but I don't see much of it
today, and when I do detect it, what a blessing it is to my own heart.

> **LORD, in trouble have they visited thee, they poured out
> a prayer when thy chastening was upon them [Isa.
> 26:16].**

In the past the remnant turned in prayer to God. Now they go back in retrospect to those difficult days:

> **Like as a woman with child, that draweth near the time of her delivery, is in pain, and crieth out in her pangs; so have we been in thy sight, O LORD [Isa. 26:17].**

In the Great Tribulation the nation Israel was like a woman in child-birth, so great was their suffering. The prophet is now looking back over that period (which is yet future). He saw it from the other side of the river of time.

> **We have been with child, we have been in pain, we have as it were brought forth wind; we have not wrought any deliverance in the earth; neither have the inhabitants of the world fallen [Isa. 26:18].**

"We have as it were brought forth wind"—that is, the suffering produced no fruitful results. This period did not change the heart of the wicked. They continued to blaspheme the God of heaven.

Today the suffering that comes to you, like a birth pang, will either bring forth something worthwhile, or it can just be wind. I am afraid many of us have suffered for *nothing*, simply because we do not see that all things work together for the glory of God. Remember that Isaiah is talking about the coming Millennium, and we could be living in a state similar to the Millennium if we would only seek Him early.

> **Thy dead men shall live, together with my dead body shall they arise. Awake and sing, ye that dwell in dust: for thy dew is as the dew of herbs, and the earth shall cast out the dead [Isa. 26:19].**

Chapter 27 concludes the threefold song of the coming of the kingdom which we have in chapters 25—27.

SONG OF THE VINEYARD

In that day the LORD with his sore and great and strong sword shall punish leviathan the piercing serpent, even leviathan that crooked serpent; and he shall slay the dragon that is in the sea [Isa. 27:1].

"In that day"—projects us immediately into the future. As we have said, this is a technical expression that refers to the Day of the Lord. It is a day that begins, as the Hebrew day did, with the evening, the time of the Great Tribulation, and it goes on into the millennial kingdom. I personally feel that it goes on into eternity, as that will be a sunrise that will never end.

"The LORD with his sore and great and strong sword." The Lord's sword is the Word of God. In describing the coming of the Lord Jesus, Revelation 1:16 says, "And he had in his right hand seven stars: and out of his mouth went a sharp two-edged sword: and his countenance was as the sun shineth in his strength." With that sword He will smite the nations. An amillennialist will say, "You say you take the Bible literally. Is this a literal sword?" Well, I've discovered that the tongue is really a sharp thing. And Hebrews 4:12 tells us, "For the word of God is quick, and powerful, and sharper than any two-edged sword . . . ." I take it that the Word of God is meant here. It is by His Word—that's all He needs. By His Word He created all things, and by His Word shall He judge.

Whom is He going to judge? "Leviathan the piercing serpent, even leviathan that crooked serpent." In that day, at the beginning of the kingdom, the Lord Jesus will bring judgment upon the serpent, leviathan, who is Satan. In Revelation 20:1-3 we are told that Satan will be shut up in the bottomless pit for one thousand years. In Revelation 12:9 we read, "And the great dragon was cast out, that old serpent, called the Devil, and Satan, which deceiveth the whole world: he was cast out into the earth, and his angels were cast out with him." Job 41:15 says of him, "His scales are his pride . . . ." The scales are for his protection, and Satan thinks he is invulnerable, that he cannot be touched. This is his pride. He doesn't realize, even today, as I understand it, that he can be judged. He probably thinks he is beyond the judgment of Almighty God.

There are a great many people today who think that there is no judgment coming. They laugh at the idea. That is the thinking of Satan, my friend.

F. Delitzsch has suggested that "the piercing serpent," or literally, "swift-fleeing serpent," represents the Tigris River and thereby the nation of Assyria. The "crooked serpent" represents the winding Euphrates and thereby the nation of Babylon. "The dragon that is in the sea" represents the Nile River and thereby the nation of Egypt. This would not militate against "leviathan," meaning Satan, but would enforce that interpretation since Satan was the power behind these kingdoms.

In that day sing unto her, A vineyard of red wine [Isa. 27:2].

Actually, I believe that chapter 27 begins with verse 2 and that verse 1 belongs with the previous chapter. However, that is a technical point with which I will not get involved. There is a change of subject at this point.

"In that day sing ye unto her." This is the Millennium, and we all can sing now—even I will be able to sing.

"A vineyard of red wine" speaks of abundance, fruitfulness, bounty, and joy. What a contrast this is to Isaiah 5! In Isaiah 5 we had the song of the vineyard, but it was a dirge. That vineyard was Israel, and God was going to bring judgment because she hadn't brought forth fruit. Here we are in the Millennium, and there is an abundance of fruit. Why?

I the LORD do keep it; I will water it every moment: lest any hurt it, I will keep it night and day [Isa. 27:3].

The Lord is the husbandman here, and never again will He ever let the vineyard out to others. He is the husbandman who keeps an eye continually upon it. He watches it night and day so that no enemy may

enter. This ought to say something to those who believe that God is
through with Israel. Scripture makes it clear that He is *not* through
with Israel.

> **Or let him take hold of my strength, that he may make
> peace with me; and he shall make peace with me [Isa.
> 27:5].**

The enemy can make peace with God even in the kingdom, for God
never ceases to be merciful. Thank God for that! He is rich in mercy,
which means that He has plenty of it. I need a lot of it myself. He is rich
in grace. We will find out that ten million years from today His grace
will still be available to us. I think we will need it even in heaven.

"That he may make peace with me." This is the only place in Scripture where it is even suggested that man can make peace with God. Of
course here it has to do with obedience to the King and not the accep-
tance of Christ as Savior. Man cannot make peace with God about the
sin question. God has already done that. Romans 5:1 says, "Therefore
being justified by faith, *we have peace* with God through our Lord
Jesus Christ" (italics mine). When you are ready to agree with God and
trust Him for what He has done through Christ on the cross, then you
will have peace. You won't have it until then. This verse is not talking
about our day but about the time of the Millennium.

SMITING OF ISRAEL AND HER ENEMIES

> **Hath he smitten him, as he smote those that smote him?
> or is he slain according to the slaughter of them that are
> slain by him? [Isa. 27:7].**

This verse poses a question that has been partially answered already
in the Book of Isaiah: Why does God judge Israel more than other nations? Light creates responsibility. In view of the fact that Israel had
more light, her sin was blacker and her punishment was greater. She
received more stripes than the nations who smote her. In Amos 3:2 we
read, "You only have I known of all the families of the earth: therefore I

will punish you for all your iniquities." Her punishment was severe, but God did not destroy Israel as He did some other nations. Psalm 118:18 tells us, "The LORD hath chastened me sore: but he hath not given me over unto death." God will *not* allow Israel to be destroyed.

> **By this therefore shall the iniquity of Jacob be purged; and this is all the fruit to take away his sin; when he maketh all the stones of the altar as chalkstones that are beaten in sunder, the groves and images shall not stand up [Isa. 27:9].**

It was not the suffering for sin that atoned for Israel's sin. The sin of Jacob was purged by a blood offering, and the sin of the nation will be expiated by the blood of Christ. Just as you were saved as a sinner, that is the way it will take place in that day. Those who say that God is through with Israel simply have not read passages of Scripture like this:

> **Yet the defenced city shall be desolate, and the habitation forsaken, and left like a wilderness: there shall the calf feed, and there shall he lie down, and consume the branches thereof.**

> **When the boughs thereof are withered, they shall be broken off: the women come, and set them on fire: for it is a people of no understanding: therefore he that made them will not have mercy on them, and he that formed them will shew them no favour [Isa. 27:10–11].**

However, the cities that Israel built are to be destroyed like any city that man builds apart from God. The great ruins in the world are the result of the judgment of Almighty God. Why? Because they rejected light. They not only rejected light, they also rejected the person of the Son of God.

> **And it shall come to pass in that day, that the LORD shall beat off from the channel of the river unto the stream of**

Egypt, and ye shall be gathered one by one, O ye children of Israel.

And it shall come to pass in that day, that the great
trumpet shall be blown, and they shall come which
were ready to perish in the land of Assyria, and the out-
casts in the land of Egypt, and shall worship the LORD in
the holy mount at Jerusalem [Isa. 27:12–13].

This section reveals that God definitely intends to restore the nation
Israel to the Promised Land, and I have no argument with those who
deny it. I just want to say this: It is not a question of whether Israel is
going to be restored to the land. It is a question of whether or not you
believe the Word of God. If you believe God's Word, what are you going
to do with a passage like this? You cannot spiritualize it, because the
prophet talks about Assyria, Egypt, Israel, and Jerusalem. These are
literal places. Israel is going to be literally restored. If you have a high
view of the inspiration of Scripture, then believe what God says.

This prophecy has never been fulfilled in the past. Its fulfillment is
yet future. My friend, when God moves the Jews into the land, God
will *move* them. When they come, they will worship Him. Just as He
called you and me, He will call them. We are not seeing the fulfillment
of this today.

CHAPTER 28

THEME: The immediate invasion of Ephraim by Assyria is a picture of the future and a warning to Jerusalem

This chapter brings us to an entirely new section. The prophecies which were totally future are included in chapters 24—27 inclusively. From chapters 28—35 we have prophecies which have a local and past fulfillment, and also there are those that reach into the future and cover the same period as in the previous section. This new section is identified by six woes, and it culminates in the great war of Armageddon in chapter 34, followed by the millennial benefits brought to the earth in chapter 35.

Now the chapter before us is a fine illustration of the combination of the near and far view, the past and future events, the local and immediate, and the general and far distant prophecies. We will see that which has been fulfilled and that which is yet to be fulfilled.

The northern kingdom of Israel, designated here by the term *Ephraim*, was soon to go into Assyrian captivity. This was a preview of the coming future day, but it was to be a warning to the southern kingdom of Judah. The first part was fulfilled when Shalmaneser, king of Assyria, invaded Ephraim in 721 B.C., overthrew the northern kingdom, and took the people into captivity.

THE IMMEDIATE CAPTIVITY OF EPHRAIM

The first woe is against the northern kingdom.

> Woe to the crown of pride, to the drunkards of Ephraim, whose glorious beauty is a fading flower, which are on the head of the fat valleys of them that are overcome with wine! [Isa. 28:1].

Ephraim and Israel are synonymous terms for the ten northern tribes, also called Samaria. The picture here of drunkards is both literal and spiritual. They were in a stupor as far as spiritual understanding was concerned. To be spiritually drunk is to be filled with pride.

Behold, the Lord hath a mighty and strong one, which as a tempest of hail and a destroying storm, as a flood of mighty waters overflowing, shall cast down to the earth with the hand [Isa. 28:2].

The Assyrian is designated here as a strong one, a destroying storm, and a flood of mighty waters.

The crown of pride, the drunkards of Ephraim, shall be trodden under feet [Isa. 28:3].

Maybe you don't like this, but God does not apologize for it; He simply tells us that this is what He did. The prophet picks up the future of the drunkard here. A high level of civilization had been developed in the northern kingdom with its comforts and outward beauty expressed in homes and gardens and trees. All you have to do to confirm this is go to the hill of Samaria and see the palace built by Omri and Ahab. This is the place where Ahab and Jezebel lived. It seems that the Lord always gives the wicked and the rich the best places to live, and I think it is poetic justice. It is not going to be so good for the wicked and rich in the next world; so they have it pretty good here. The hill of Samaria is one of the most beautiful spots in the land. When I stood there I could see the Mediterranean Sea, the Jordan valley, Mount Hermon in the north covered with snow, and the walls of Jerusalem in the south. My friend, you could not ask for a more beautiful place to live. If a real estate man develops that hill and sells lots, I hope I can buy one and build a house there. It's a great place, but God judged these people in the northern kingdom, and He brought down their high civilization.

THE FAR DISTANT JUDGMENT

Now the prophet begins to move into the future. The expression "in that day" refers to the Day of the Lord, which begins with the Great Tribulation and extends on through the Millennium.

> In that day shall the LORD of hosts be for a crown of glory, and for a diadem of beauty, unto the residue of his people [Isa. 28:5].

This looks into the future to the millennial kingdom which is coming. The thing that caused the downfall of Ephraim, the northern kingdom, was their pride—they wore a crown of pride. But in that future day when God brings them back to the land, it will be a crown of glory.

> And for a spirit of judgment to him that sitteth in judgment, and for strength to them that turn the battle to the gate.

> But they also have erred through wine, and through strong drink are out of the way; the priest and the prophet have erred through strong drink, they are swallowed up of wine, they are out of the way through strong drink; they err in vision, they stumble in judgment [Isa. 28:6–7].

A businessman recently told me some of the things that go on in big business. I don't suppose there is a day that goes by that he doesn't make deals with men who make big investments for large profits. He told me about one of these men who was beginning to indulge in sin. He was not faithful to his wife, and he was drinking heavily. He has recently made certain judgments about investments that have caused this businessman to withhold loaning money to him. He told me that when a man begins to drink and indulge in sin he loses his sharpness in business. He said, "Because I am a Christian I may be biased, but I have found over the long haul, over a period of years, that this is factual. I have learned it through bitter experiences."

Now God is making this same observation regarding the northern kingdom: "they are out of the way through strong drink; they err in vision, they stumble in judgment."

> **But the word of the LORD was unto them precept upon precept, precept upon precept; line upon line, line upon line; here a little, and there a little; that they might go, and fall backward, and be broken, and snared, and taken [Isa. 28:13].**

Sections like this have caused some expositors of the past to call Isaiah "the prophet of the commonplace." Teaching is a slow, patient, and continuous work. This is the way that even spiritual truth is imparted. God does not impart it in a flash to a lazy and lethargic soul As the people lapse into apostasy in any age, it becomes increasingly difficult to impart spiritual truth.

There are many Christians today who are not satisfied with their Christian lives. To be brutally frank, they are ignorant of the Word of God. Then they hear about a wonderful two-week course that will give them the answers to all their problems. They will learn how to handle their marital problems, how to get along with their mother-in-law, how to guide their children aright, and how to become model employees. My friend, let me say this to you very candidly. Neither a little course nor some great emotional experience will solve your problems. There is no shortcut to success in the Christian life. There is only one way to grow as a Christian, and it is so commonplace and ordinary that I hesitate to say it. The Word of the Lord was given unto Israel precept upon precept, line upon line, here a little, and there a little. It was the daily grind of getting into God's Word. What happened? Israel did not follow through. They fell backward; that is, they were in a backslidden state. There are many Christians in the same condition today. It is not that they are weaker than anybody else; it is simply that they do not spend enough time in the Word of God. I realize that this method is not very exciting, but line upon line and precept upon precept is the only way you are going to grow in the Christian life.

THE WARNING TO JUDAH

Wherefore hear the word of the LORD, ye scornful men, that rule this people which is in Jerusalem [Isa. 28:14].

The judgment coming to Israel in the north should be a warning to Judah in the south. Ephraim speaks to Jerusalem, Jerusalem speaks to us today, and the Word of God speaks to all of us. It looks as if God wrote this Book, not yesterday, but tomorrow. In fact, it is way ahead of tomorrow's newspaper.

Because ye have said, We have made a covenant with death, and with hell are we at agreement; when the overflowing scourge shall pass through, it shall not come unto us: for we have made lies our refuge, and under falsehood have we hid ourselves [Isa. 28:15].

What is this covenant with death and Sheol? Daniel tells us about a future covenant which Israel will make with the Antichrist, the prince who is coming, the Man of Sin, the godless man, the willful king, the beast out of the sea and the beast out of the land, the one who is controlled by Satan (see Dan. 9:27).

Therefore thus saith the Lord GOD, Behold, I lay in Zion for a foundation a stone, a tried stone, a precious corner stone, a sure foundation: he that believeth shall not make haste [Isa. 28:16].

What is the answer today to the falsehood in the lives of people and the deception that is abroad which will continue to snowball right on down into the Great Tribulation Period? Well, God has already put that answer down. It is a foundation; it is a tried stone, a precious cornerstone, a sure foundation. One who believes in it doesn't need to be in a hurry. He can rest in Him. First Peter 2:6–8 speaks of Him: "Wherefore also it is contained in the scripture, Behold, I lay in Sion a chief corner stone, elect, precious; and he that believeth on him shall not be confounded. Unto you therefore which believe he is precious: but unto them which be disobedient, the stone which the builders disallowed, the same is made the head of the corner, And a stone of stumbling, and a rock of offence, even to them which stumble at the word, being disobedient: whereunto also they were appointed." Simon Peter makes it very clear that this stone is Christ.

> **Judgment also will I lay to the line, and righteousness to the plummet: and the hail shall sweep away the refuge of lies, and the waters shall overflow the hiding place [Isa. 28:17].**

Judgment for these people is going to come gradually. I think it comes that way today. Sometimes it comes suddenly. But gradual judgment is worse than sudden judgment, for usually the process is so slow that you don't detect it.

> **For the bed is shorter than that a man can stretch himself on it: and the covering narrower than that he can wrap himself in it [Isa. 28:20].**

Have you ever gone to a hotel or a motel and found that the covers on the bed were not quite long enough? They don't come up to your neck, and if you pull them up, then your feet stick out. Have you ever slept in a short bed, where your feet hang over the edge, or you have to prop your head up, or you have to sleep at an angle? That's not so good, is it? God says to these people, "I am giving you a short bed. The cover won't be quite long enough." From then on the judgment of God will come. It didn't come to Judah for about one hundred years, but it finally came.

THE FINAL JUDGMENT OF GOD UPON HIS PEOPLE

The remainder of this chapter is almost the parable of the wheat and the tares. He talks about the different kinds of grain, the hard grains and the soft grains, and the different methods of threshing it.

> **When he hath made plain the face thereof, doth he not cast abroad the fitches, and scatter the cummin, and cast in the principal wheat and the appointed barley and the rie in their place? [Isa. 28:25].**

The grains are "fitches" (sometimes translated *fennel* or *dill*), "cummin, wheat, barley, and rie."

> **For the fitches are not threshed with a threshing instrument, neither is a cart wheel turned about upon the cummin; but the fitches are beaten out with a staff, and the cummin with a rod.**
>
> **Bread corn is bruised; because he will not ever be threshing it, nor break it with the wheel of his cart, nor bruise it with his horsemen [Isa. 28:27-28].**

A farmer has to be careful about the way he harvests soft grains. Each grain is different.

Now he says that this is the way God judges. Judgment is spoken of as the harvest. The individual or nation actually determines the character of the judgment which is to fall upon them. In other words, if you are hard and resist God, you are a hard grain. You are a hard nut to crack, and the judgment is going to be severe for you. A man came to me and told me that he had lost his wife and two children before he came to himself. He said, "God had to knock me down *three* times because I was such a hardened sinner." God will thresh you; and, if you are hard, the judgment will be hard.

The Lord Jesus put it like this in Matthew 13:30, "Let both grow together until the harvest: and in the time of harvest I will say to the reapers, Gather ye together first the tares, and bind them in bundles to burn them: but gather the wheat into my barn." In Matthew 13:41 the Lord goes on to say, "The Son of man shall send forth his angels, and they shall gather out of his kingdom all things that offend, and them which do iniquity." How tremendous this is! We ourselves determine our own judgment. If we only will listen to Him, He will put us over where the wheat is and spare us the severity of His judgment.

CHAPTER 29

THEME: Jerusalem—prophecies of immediate future and reaching on into the kingdom

The prophecies in this chapter are confined to Jerusalem but extend from the invasion of Sennacherib through the time when Jerusalem will be trodden down of the Gentiles until the last invader (see Zech. 14:1–7) shall have destroyed Jerusalem and, finally, to the establishment of the kingdom when the Messiah shall come and His feet shall touch the Mount of Olives.

It will prove profitable to compare this chapter with our Lord's discourse on Jerusalem in Matthew 23:37—24:2 and with Luke 13:34–35; 21:20–24.

JERUSALEM—HISTORY AND PROPHECY

Woe to Ariel, to Ariel, the city where David dwelt! add ye year to year; let them kill sacrifices [Isa. 29:1].

It is necessary to establish the fact that Jerusalem is the city designated under the title of Ariel. *Ariel* means "lionlike." The word occurs in 2 Samuel 23:20 which says, "And Benaiah the son of Jehoiada, the son of a valiant man, of Kabzeel, who had done many acts, he slew two lionlike men of Moab. . . ." A lionlike man is an "Ariel" man. The word also carries the meaning of "the lion of God." In Ezekiel 43:16 the same word is translated "altar" and, under certain circumstances, could mean "the altar of God." Both designations are a fitting title for the city of Jerusalem. It is further identified here as "the city where David dwelt." The lion is the insignia of that family. Our Lord is called the ". . . Lion of the tribe of Juda" (Rev. 5:5). Likewise Jerusalem was the place where the temple of God was, and the altar, of course, was there.

This is a remarkable prophecy concerning Jerusalem. The prophecy began to be fulfilled in Isaiah's day and has continued right down to today. If you walk down the streets of Jerusalem, you will see this prophecy being fulfilled, and it will continue to be fulfilled.

> **Yet I will distress Ariel, and there shall be heaviness and sorrow: and it shall be unto me as Ariel [Isa. 29:2].**

This is judgment upon Jerusalem.

> **And I will camp against thee round about, and will lay siege against thee with a mount, and I will raise forts against thee.**

> **And thou shalt be brought down, and shalt speak out of the ground, and thy speech shall be low out of the dust, and thy voice shall be, as of one that hath a familiar spirit, out of the ground, and thy speech shall whisper out of the dust.**

> **Moreover the multitude of thy strangers shall be like small dust, and the multitude of the terrible ones shall be as chaff that passeth away: yea, it shall be at an instant suddenly [Isa. 29:3–5].**

This prophecy was given before Nebuchadnezzar came up to the city of Jerusalem and destroyed it, which marked the beginning of the ". . . times of the Gentiles . . ." (Luke 21:24). Our Lord said that Jerusalem would be trodden down of the Gentiles until the Time of the Gentiles be fulfilled. The Gentiles have marched through her streets and still do today.

Jerusalem has been besieged and captured more often than any other city. I have in my files a list of twenty-seven sieges that have been leveled against this city throughout history. Almost every time it was taken, it was destroyed. That is why it is not quite accurate for people to say, "Go to Jerusalem and walk where Jesus walked." You are not going to walk where He walked, because Jerusalem is much higher today than it was in His day. For example, the pool of Bethesda was about fifty feet down from the level of the ground today. The Lord Jesus walked down there. It is quite evident that Solomon's temple was probably more than one hundred feet beneath where the Mosque of Omar stands today. The city has been destroyed many times, and each time it was leveled off and rebuilt on the wreckage. That is what Nehemiah did—out of the debris and wreckage he rebuilt the walls of Jerusalem. Rocks did not have to be hauled in for repair work because there are more rocks over there than they could ever use. I heard a few years ago that stones were being shipped from Indiana to Jerusalem to rebuild the temple. That report was proven false, but how foolish it would have been. There is no place on the topside of this earth that is as rocky as Jerusalem and the surrounding area. It is a rugged terrain. That is one reason Jerusalem was so difficult for the enemy to take.

> Thou shalt be visited of the LORD of hosts with thunder, and with earthquake, and great noise, with storm and tempest, and the flame of devouring fire.

> And the multitude of all the nations that fight against Ariel, even all that fight against her and her munition, and that distress her, shall be as a dream of a night vision.

> It shall even be as when an hungry man dreameth, and, behold, he eateth; but he awaketh, and his soul is empty: or as when a thirsty man dreameth, and, behold, he drinketh; but he awaketh, and, behold, he is faint, and his soul hath appetite: so shall the multitude of all the nations be, that fight against mount Zion [Isa. 29:6-8].

The final siege of Jerusalem will be the worst of all (see Zech. 14), but God will intervene at the last moment and deliver His people from extermination. All the dreams of the enemies of God to bring in their own kingdom will be frustrated, and God will put them down. He will build His own kingdom and establish it Himself, just as He said He would do.

JERUSALEM—MEANING AND MESSAGE

Stay yourselves, and wonder; cry ye out, and cry: they are drunken, but not with wine; they stagger, but not with strong drink.

For the LORD hath poured out upon you the spirit of deep sleep, and hath closed your eyes: the prophets and your rulers, the seers hath he covered [Isa. 29:9–10].

I have said that Isaiah is the prophet of the commonplace, and what he says fits into our contemporary culture. Did God actually make them sleepy? How did He do it? He kept giving Israel light; and, as He gave them light, they kept rejecting it. They would not accept the truth that He gave them. They could not see it, which revealed that they were blind. That is the way God puts people to sleep and the way He reveals that they are blind. Even the prophets and princes did not anticipate this deliverance from God. They were as blinded to the future as the enemies of God. They were as men who were dead drunk.

And the vision of all is become unto you as the words of a book that is sealed, which men deliver to one that is learned, saying, Read this, I pray thee: and he saith, I cannot; for it is sealed:

And the book is delivered to him that is not learned, saying, Read this, I pray thee: and he saith, I am not learned [Isa. 29:11–12].

The attitude of the people, including God's people, before their final deliverance by God was that prophecy was too obscure to be understood, that it was a sealed subject about which they could know nothing. This is the present-day attitude of many church leaders and preachers. I have heard seminary professors and ministers say, "Well, you know, the Book of Revelation is a sealed book. Nobody can understand it." Those who insist that Revelation is a sealed book and that we are not supposed to understand it are saying exactly what the people in Isaiah's day were saying about prophecy. Or, people today will say that they are too busy, that they don't have time to study the Word of God. All kinds of excuses are offered by Christians for their own ignorance of the Scriptures.

The word *revelation* is from the Greek word *apocalypse*, which means "unveiled." God took the seal from the Book of Revelation so that it *can* be understood. In one sense Revelation is the simplest book in the Bible, but you must have an understanding of the sixty-five books that precede it. It is the last book of the Bible, and certainly it is not the place you should begin reading. No book is so organized, and I found it to be the easiest book in the Bible to outline. It is nonsense to say that it is symbolic, a sealed book that we are not supposed to understand. That is what they were saying in Isaiah's day. God will judge you for that kind of thinking because when He gives light and you will not open your eyes, you become blind to the light. Listen to what God says of Revelation in Revelation 1:3, "Blessed is he that readeth, and they that hear the words of this prophecy, and keep those things which are written therein: for the time is at hand." Revelation 22:10 says, "And he saith unto me, Seal not the saying of the prophecy of this book: for the time is at hand." It is *not* a sealed book.

Wherefore the Lord said, Forasmuch as this people draw near me with their mouth, and with their lips do honour me, but have removed their heart far from me, and their fear toward me is taught by the precept of men [Isa. 29:13].

If you had lived in Isaiah's day, you would have wondered what Isaiah really meant because the people were going to the temple. It was crowded—anytime a sacrifice was offered you would find people there. There was a place for the men, a court for the women, and a court for the Gentiles. Why was God finding fault with these people? They were all coming to church, but they went through all of the ritual with their mouths. It was as if they could say the Lord's Prayer and the Apostles' Creed, but it did not mean anything to them. They did not believe what they were saying; they did not accept God's Word. God said that their hearts were far from Him. That is the reason He judged them, and that is the reason He is going to judge us today.

The curse of the world today is religion. God would like you to get rid of religion and come to Christ. Religion is the greatest barrier for many people today. I made that statement to a man not long ago. Immediately he countered by saying, "I want you to know, Dr. McGee, that I am a religious man. I am religious by nature." He had a fallen nature, but he had a religious nature. I think I shocked him when I told him that he ought to get rid of his religion and that I was not a religious man. He said, "I cannot believe that there is a preacher who is not religious. If you are not religious, what are you then?" I told him that I am a sinner who came to Christ and that I have a personal relationship with Him today. It is not a religion but a relationship. Do you have Christ, or don't you? That is the important thing.

Woe unto them that seek deep to hide their counsel from the LORD, and their works are in the dark, and they say, Who seeth us? and who knoweth us? [Isa. 29:15].

Things are so serious for His people that He puts in another "Woe" here. This chapter contains two woes because (1) the people act as if God does not see or know, and (2) they act as if they are getting by with it.

JERUSALEM—HONOR AND GLORY

Is it not yet a very little while, and Lebanon shall be turned into a fruitful field, and the fruitful field shall be esteemed as a forest? [Isa. 29:17].

Now we see into the future. The time will come when there will be honor and glory in Jerusalem and in the land. God is not through with that city. Today it looks like a layer cake with one city built on top of the other. God had judged them, and He will judge them again. But Jerusalem will be rebuilt once again, and then it will be the city of God.

> And in that day shall the deaf hear the words of the
> book, and the eyes of the blind shall see out of obscurity,
> and out of darkness [Isa. 29:18].

The deaf are going to hear, and the blind are going to see.

> The meek also shall increase their joy in the LORD, and
> the poor among men shall rejoice in the Holy One of Is-
> rael [Isa. 29:19].

You have heard the old bromide, "No one is so blind as those who will
not see." Today, as in Isaiah's day, there is a willful blindness. In that
day, in the Millennium, they are going to see.

> Therefore thus saith the LORD, who redeemed Abraham,
> concerning the house of Jacob, Jacob shall not now be
> ashamed, neither shall his face now wax pale.

> But when he seeth his children, the work of mine hands,
> in the midst of him, they shall sanctify my name, and
> sanctify the Holy One of Jacob, and shall fear the God of
> Israel.

> They also that erred in spirit shall come to understand-
> ing, and they that murmured shall learn doctrine [Isa.
> 29:22-24].

What are they going to do with the name of God? They are going to
make it holy—they are going to set it apart as something wonderful.
Today, God's people, by their lives, should sanctify the name of God. It
is a holy name—but do we treat it that way?

CHAPTERS 30 AND 31

THEME: Judah admonished not to turn to Egypt for help against Assyria; exhorted to turn to the Lord.

These two chapters present largely a local situation, although a larger prophecy of a future time grows out of it. The local prophecy has been literally fulfilled. The southern kingdom of Judah heard and heeded the prophet's warning and did not join with Egypt in order to be delivered from the Assyrian. The northern kingdom of Israel made the mistake of ignoring the prophet's warning, and they went into Assyrian captivity (see 2 Kings 17:4). This is one time when the southern kingdom profited by the experience of the northern kingdom.

ADMONITION NOT TO SEEK
ALLIANCE WITH EGYPT

Woe to the rebellious children, saith the LORD, that take counsel, but not of me; and that cover with a covering, but not of my spirit, that they may add sin to sin [Isa. 30:1].

This is the fourth woe. It is a woe because it is a warning. God says in effect, "Don't go to Egypt for help, because it won't be a good thing for you to do. Help down there is a mirage on the desert."

For the Egyptians shall help in vain, and to no purpose: therefore have I cried concerning this, Their strength is to sit still [Isa. 30:7].

EXHORTATION TO TURN TO JEHOVAH
FOR DELIVERANCE

God says, "Turn to Me, and I will deliver you" (see v. 15). This is a marvelous verse, one of the gems of Scripture.

> And therefore will the LORD wait, that he may be gracious unto you, and therefore will he be exalted, that he may have mercy upon you: for the LORD is a God of judgment: blessed are all they that wait for him [Isa. 30:18].

Don't be in a hurry. Don't say, "We are at the end of the age, and the Lord is going to come this year or next—or at least before the year two thousand." God says, "Let Me work this out. I have not given you any dates." Learn to wait upon the Lord. This matter of looking for the Lord Jesus to come to take His own out of the world is a matter of *waiting*. And we are told that they who wait on the Lord will renew their strength. You cannot rush God. He is in no hurry. Maybe things are not working out the way you think they should; maybe you and I would like to rearrange them, but let God work things out. He has eternity ahead of Him; and, when you and I get in step with Him, life will be much easier for us down here.

DECLARATION THAT GOD WILL DEAL
WITH THE FINAL ASSYRIAN

> For through the voice of the LORD shall the Assyrian be beaten down, which smote with a rod.

> And in every place where the grounded staff shall pass, which the LORD shall lay upon him, it shall be with tabrets and harps: and in battles of shaking will he fight with it.

> For Tophet is ordained of old; yea, for the king it is prepared; he hath made it deep and large: the pile thereof is fire and much wood; the breath of the LORD, like a stream of brimstone, doth kindle it [Isa. 30:31–33].

The Assyrian here is the final enemy of God in the Great Tribulation. "Tophet" was a place in the valley of the son of Hinnom where the most abominable idolatries were practiced. Little children were offered as sacrifices! It speaks in this passage of the worst spot in the lake of fire.

"The king" mentioned represents the beast and the false prophet: "And the devil that deceived them was cast into the lake of fire and brimstone, where the beast and the false prophet are, and shall be tormented day and night for ever and ever" (Rev. 20:10).

In chapter 31 the prophet warns God's people again not to look to Egypt for help but to trust the Lord to defend Jerusalem. So pressing is the danger, and so evident is the likelihood of the Israelites turning to Egypt, that Isaiah continues to warn Judah of the futility of such a measure. In the future Israel will turn to the wrong ally. They will accept the Antichrist, and God is warning them about it here. God will judge those who turn to outside help instead of to Him.

> **Woe to them that go down to Egypt for help; and stay on horses, and trust in chariots, because they are many; and in horsemen, because they are very strong; but they look not unto the Holy One of Israel, neither seek the LORD! [Isa. 31:1].**

This is the fifth woe. It is pronounced on those who go down to Egypt for help.

This has a message for you and me. Woe to you and woe to me when we turn away from God and turn to some materialistic or human help. Don't misunderstand me—He doesn't intend that you launch out into space and hang there. God expects you to be reasonable. But in the final analysis God wants top priority as far as giving help is concerned. My friend, where do you go for help? To your banker? To your preacher? Every now and then I receive a letter from someone who asks me what he should do in a given situation. Well, I don't know what to do with many problems that arise in my own life! Although it is nice to ask others for advice, in the final analysis we must go to God for help. The psalmist wrote: "Some trust in chariots, and some in horses: but we will remember the name of the LORD our God (Ps. 20:7).

Materialistic philosophy says that it is smart to trust in the stock market or your investments, that it is smart to look to "Egypt." Most of us have some "Egypt" upon which we depend for help. The real source of Israel's difficulty was that they did not look to God, nor did they seek Him. Since they did not trust Him, they turned frantically to some outside, physical display of power.

As birds flying, so will the LORD of hosts defend Jerusalem: defending also he will deliver it; and passing over he will preserve it [Isa. 31:5].

The Lord will defend and preserve Jerusalem in the days of Hezekiah, as we shall see. God assures them that it is a sure thing that the Assyrians will not take the city of Jerusalem.

Then shall the Assyrian fall with the sword, not of a mighty man; and the sword, not of a mean man, shall devour him: but he shall flee from the sword, and his young men shall be discomfited [Isa. 31:8].

"Not of a mighty man"—God says it is not because you are going to be strong enough to drive them away. You won't. God will deal with the Assyrians. Jerusalem's confidence should be in the Lord.

This is a great chapter to read for our own help and strength.

CHAPTER 32

THEME: The coming King, the coming Tribulation, and the coming Spirit

This chapter is a bright note between the fifth and sixth woes; it is a ray of light to God's people in a dark place in that day.

It has been some time since the person of the King has been before us, but we find Him introduced again at this point, for there can be no Millennium or blessing to this earth without Him.

THE KING WHO IS TO REIGN

Behold, a king shall reign in righteousness, and princes shall rule in judgment [Isa. 32:1].

This verse projects into the kingdom age. The King is none other than the Lord Jesus Christ. The character of His reign is righteousness. The world has never had a kingdom like this so far.

And a man shall be as an hiding place from the wind, and a covert from the tempest; as rivers of water in a dry place, as the shadow of a great rock in a weary land [Isa. 32:2].

The Lord is not only King, He is also a Savior-King. He bore the winds and tempest of the judgment of sin for us. He is a Rock for our protection. He was set before us in Isaiah 26:4 as the Rock of ages. This is another aspect of His ministry under the figure of the rock. He is a place of hiding for believers in our day also.

And the eyes of them that see shall not be dim, and the ears of them that hear shall hearken [Isa. 32:3].

In other words, there will be spiritual understanding given to all of God's people. "For now we see through a glass, darkly; but then face to face . . ." (1 Cor. 13:12). True spiritual values will then be ascertained and made obvious. And that which should have top priority *will* have top priority. In our day moral values are gone. One of the great problems in this country is that we have lost the sense of moral values. For many years now our schools have been teaching the evolutionary theory which makes man an animal. Moral values are not taught. If you advocate law and order and a high state of morality, you are considered a square, a back number, and somehow not as smart as are the sophisticated and clever crooks. Therefore, the feeling is, "Let's not listen to that old stuff." Well, the "old stuff" is going to be the future stuff also, because the earth will have a King reigning in righteousness. Then the moral values will come back into place.

The vile person shall be no more called liberal, nor the churl said to be bountiful [Isa. 32:5].

I love this—it is about as up to date as we can get. We have today what are known as the limousine liberals. The rich, for the most part, are liberal. Why? They already have their wealth which is not being taxed, but the middle man is being taxed unmercifully to pay for new projects that the rich are promoting. You can be sure of one thing: the rich man could afford to be liberal. Lazarus sat on the floor and caught the crumbs that fell from the rich man's table. That rich man was liberal—he was very liberal with his crumbs—but that was all.

In our day a "vile person" is "called liberal." In that day a vile person will no longer be called liberal, because he will be seen for what he really is. He is a villain, and his heart will work iniquity. The human heart is desperately wicked. Everything in that future day will be seen in its true colors. There will be no false values. Every man will be seen for what he is. There will be no "putting on a front" or assuming what they are not. The mask of hypocrisy will be removed. This, of course, applies to everyone—not only to Christians. The biggest hypocrites are actually not in the church. They are all those who pretend to be something they are not.

All of this will take place when the King comes who will reign in righteousness.

THE PRECEDING TIME OF TROUBLE

Before Christ, the King, comes to reign, there will be a time of trouble, which will be the Great Tribulation.

> **Rise up, ye women that are at ease; hear my voice, ye careless daughters; give ear unto my speech [Isa. 32:9].**

Why does he say this? Because naturally women are more sensitive than men, and they sense danger before a man does. My friend, every man before he goes into business partnership or any kind of partnership should let his wife meet the person who is to be his partner. She is apt to give him a true evaluation of his nature and character. In my home I try to maintain my place as the head of the house, but I have discovered over a period of years that I am no judge of human character. Time after time my wife has said to me, "Well, you misjudged that person." Either I put confidence in someone when I should not have, or I failed to recognize that certain people are really wonderful folk. So I have learned that the best thing to do is to listen to her, especially in the evaluation of character. Now God says that in the days prior to the Tribulation Period women will become so insensible that they will not recognize the danger that is coming. It is quite interesting that there will be women living in pleasure in that day to such extent that they will have no sense of coming judgment.

THE PROMISE OF THE SPIRIT

Now we come to the third division: the promise of the Spirit to be poured out in the last days.

> **Until the spirit be poured upon us from on high, and the wilderness be a fruitful field, and the fruitful field be counted for a forest [Isa. 32:15].**

Here is a case where you need to pay attention to the development of prophecy in the Word of God. When will the Spirit be poured out? The Spirit will be poured out during the Millennium when Christ reigns. That is going to be the greatest time of spiritual blessing and turning to Christ, for at that time He will be reigning in person. That doesn't mean that every knee is going to bow to Him at that time. Every knee will bow to Him eventually, but the kingdom will be a time of testing. Joel mentions it: "And it shall come to pass afterward, that I will pour out my spirit upon all flesh; and your sons and your daughters shall prophesy, your old men shall dream dreams, your young men shall see visions: And also upon the servants and upon the handmaids in those days will I pour out my spirit" (Joel 2:28–29). This looks forward to the coming kingdom. This prophecy was not fulfilled at Pentecost nor any time since then.

In Acts 2:15–21 Peter quotes from Joel 2:28–29 and explains the passage. Peter did not say that Pentecost was a fulfillment of the prophecy in Joel, but that Pentecost was similar to what Joel described. The people who were filled with the Holy Spirit in Peter's day were ridiculed as being drunk early in the morning. Now that could happen in Los Angeles today, but people did not get drunk in the morning in Peter's day. Peter was saying that what was happening at Pentecost was similar to what would take place during the millennial kingdom.

What Joel and Peter described will take place during the kingdom age when the Lord pours out His Spirit upon all flesh. On the Day of Pentecost it was poured out on only a few people, but it was similar to that which will occur during the Millennium.

Joel's prediction was of tremendous phenomena: "And I will shew wonders in the heavens and the earth, blood, and fire, and pillars of smoke. The sun shall be turned into darkness, and the moon into blood, before the great and the terrible day of the LORD come" (Joel 2:30–31). My friend, these tremendous signs have never yet taken place.

Notice also that Joel predicted, ". . . and your sons and your daughters shall prophesy, your old men shall dream dreams . . ." (Joel 2:28). Today our young people are not fulfilling this prophecy, and our old men are in a retirement place playing golf. These things did not happen on the Day of Pentecost, neither are they happening today. This prophecy looks forward to the coming kingdom. There is always a danger of pulling out a few verses of Scripture and trying to build on them a system of prophecy. We are just to let the Word of God speak to us—line upon line and precept upon precept—as He wants to do it. This is the way God gives it to us.

CHAPTER 33

THEME: The final woe is pronounced on all who spoil God's people and land

This chapter, in particular, pronounces a judgment upon those who seek to destroy God's people and lay waste His land. It refers to the Assyrians in the immediate purview but extends to the final enemy of the last days. The chapter is geocentric. The land is the thing of primary importance.

PRAYER OF THE REMNANT FOR DELIVERANCE

Woe to thee that spoilest, and thou wast not spoiled; and dealest treacherously, and they dealt not treacherously with thee! when thou shalt cease to spoil, thou shalt be spoiled; and when thou shalt make an end to deal treacherously, they shall deal treacherously with thee [Isa. 33:1].

This is Isaiah's way of expressing the great spiritual principles, which God put down from the time man sinned. It is stated well in Galatians 6:7: "Be not deceived; God is not mocked: for whatsoever a man soweth, that shall he also reap."

The "spoiler" here is Sennacherib who came against Jerusalem during the reign of Hezekiah (Isa. 36—37). I believe this is the unanimous conclusion of all sound scholars. However, it does not limit this chapter to the Assyrians. God says in effect, "You spoil My people, and I'll spoil you." God promises to take vengeance on behalf of His people. For this reason we as believers should always let God handle all of our revenge. God says that we are not to avenge ourselves, but He will repay. Turn it over to God. He can do a better job than we can do.

Now this is also a picture of that final day of consummation after God has brought together again the restored Roman Empire, and Anti-

christ will destroy the land of Israel again. God will take care of him at
the second coming of Christ.

Now in view of that, we hear this prayer:

> **O LORD, be gracious unto us; we have waited for thee: be
> thou their arm every morning, our salvation also in the
> time of trouble [Isa. 33:2].**

This is the prayer of the godly remnant then and in the future.

PLAINTIVE CRY OF AMBASSADORS WHO FAILED

> **Behold their valiant ones shall cry without: the ambas-
> sadors of peace shall weep bitterly.**

> **The highways lie waste, the wayfaring man ceaseth: he
> hath broken the covenant, he hath despised the cities, he
> regardeth no man [Isa. 33:7-8].**

You would think that we would have learned a lesson today, but we
have not. A great peace conference was held at the Hague; and, while
it was going on, Germany began World War I and broke all of the trea-
ties. At the end of that war the League of Nations was formed; and,
when President Woodrow Wilson went to be our representative, the
idea was to make the world safe for democracy. What they forgot, however, was to make democracy safe for the world. Peace didn't come. It
led to World War II. Now the United Nations is making the world ready
for World War III. We talk about peace, but we are not doing it God's
way.

PETITION FOR ALL TO CONSIDER
GOD'S DEALINGS

> **Hear, ye that are far off, what I have done; and, ye that
> are near, acknowledge my spirit [Isa. 33:13].**

Two groups of people are addressed here: "Ye that are far off" are the Gentiles, and "ye that are near" are the people of Israel. The call is to recognize God.

> The sinners in Zion are afraid; fearfulness hath surprised the hypocrites. Who among us shall dwell with the devouring fire? who among us shall dwell with everlasting burnings? [Isa. 33:14].

"Sinners in Zion" are those of Israel who are not Israel. There are godless Israelites just as there are godless Gentiles.

"The devouring fire" does not refer to the lake of fire mentioned in the Book of Revelation, but rather to the fact that "our God is a consuming fire." He is a holy God, and He intends to judge in that day.

Today there is a tremendous godless movement abroad. It is growing by leaps and bounds. That is the reason we are giving out the Word of God. We don't know how much longer we can do it, but we are going to continue as long as the Lord allows. God is going to bring judgment, and God's people need to be concerned about getting His Word out. Judgment is not a pretty subject. It is not one that will make friends, but these are the words of Isaiah, and Isaiah's message is God's message, and He would like the human family to hear it.

> He that walketh righteously, and speaketh uprightly; he that despiseth the gain of oppressions, that shaketh his hands from holding of bribes, that stoppeth his ears from hearing of blood, and shutteth his eyes from seeing evil [Isa. 33:15].

The one who has been declared righteous by his faith in Christ is called to walk in righteousness. In that awful day we find that where sin abounds, grace will much more abound.

PRAISE TO GOD FOR FINAL DELIVERANCE

Now we come to the fourth division, where there is praise to God for final deliverance.

> Look upon Zion, the city of our solemnities: thine eyes
> shall see Jerusalem a quiet habitation, a tabernacle
> that shall not be taken down; not one of the stakes
> thereof shall ever be removed, neither shall any of the
> cords thereof be broken.
>
> But there the glorious LORD will be unto us a place of
> broad rivers and streams; wherein shall go no galley
> with oars, neither shall gallant ship pass thereby [Isa.
> 33:20–21].

Babylon could boast of the Euphrates River, Assyria could boast of the Tigris and upper Zab, and Egypt could boast of the Nile, but Jerusalem was a landlocked city with neither river nor harbor. However, Zechariah gave an amazing prophecy which leads us to believe that God will provide a harbor for Israel during the Millennium (see Zech. 14:4–8). It is my understanding that the earthquake he describes will open up a deep valley to the Mediterranean Sea, and Jerusalem will be a seaport town during the Millennium.

The literal fulfillment of the prophecy also has a spiritual application. "The glorious LORD will be unto us a place of broad rivers and streams." The Lord Himself is the source of Israel's defense and blessing.

> And the inhabitant shall not say, I am sick: the people
> that dwell therein shall be forgiven their iniquity [Isa.
> 33:24].

This is a glorious prospect which is held out for Jerusalem. The eye of faith looks beyond the immediate hard circumstances to the glorious prospect of the future. This is the day when the King will be in Jerusalem. The Prince of peace will then bring peace to the earth.

CHAPTER 34

THEME: The final world clash—the Battle of
Armageddon

This chapter brings to an end the section which in my outline I call
the "Kingdom, Process, and Program by which the Throne is Established on Earth." Judgment has been the theme all the way through
this section. We have looked at six woes and followed a progression in
this matter of prophecy. We saw a local situation into which Isaiah
spoke and then watched him move into that broader area, as he looked
down through the centuries to the time of judgment that was coming
in the future, which the Lord Jesus called the Great Tribulation. Beyond that we saw the coming of the King.

However, in our day we are not looking for the King, we are looking
for our Savior. We are "Looking for that blessed hope, and the glorious
appearing of the great God and our Saviour Jesus Christ" (Titus 2:13).
After He takes the church out of the world, those who remain will go
through the frightful Tribulation Period, which will end with the war
or the campaign of Armageddon.

This chapter is in contradiction to the philosophy of the world. You
see, man expects to so improve the world by his own efforts that he
will build a Utopia. He plans to bring in a millennium, although he
may call it something else. Man thinks he is capable of lifting himself
by his own bootstraps. The basic philosophy of evolution (and evolution is a philosophy rather than a science) is that there is improvement
as we go along. It is onward and upward forever! Or, as the slogan has
it, "Every day in every way I am getting better and better." Man has
woven this philosophy into the fabric of life; he thinks we are moving
into something which is great and good.

The Word of God also looks forward to a wonderful future for this
earth, but it is not the consummation of man's efforts. Everything that
man has built apart from God is coming under a frightful judgment.
All of man's work is contrary to God and must come into a final con-

flict. That conflict is set before us here as the Battle of Armageddon.
The sin of man will finally be headed up in the Man of Sin, who will
attempt to bring in a kingdom for himself, and that kingdom is the
Great Tribulation Period. It can only be ended with the coming of
Christ to the earth to establish His kingdom.

This chapter looks entirely to the future. The Assyrians have disappeared, F. Delitzsch has made this statement, which I think is quite
accurate: "We feel that we are carried away from the stage of history,
and are transported into the midst of the last things," and these chapters are the "last steps whereby our prophet rises to the height at which
he soars in chapters 40 to the end. After the fall of Assyria, and when
darkness began to gather on the horizon again, Isaiah broke away from
his own time—'the end of all things' became more and more his
home. . . . It was the revelation of the mystery of the incarnation of
God, for which all this was to prepare the way."

> **Come near, ye nations, to hear; and hearken, ye people:
> let the earth hear, and all that is therein; the world, and
> all things that come forth of it [Isa. 34:1].**

In Isaiah 1:2 God called heaven and earth to witness His judgment
upon His people Israel. In this chapter God calls only the nations of
the earth to witness His final judgment upon the nations.

> **For the indignation of the LORD is upon all nations, and
> his fury upon all their armies: he hath utterly destroyed
> them, he hath delivered them to the slaughter [Isa.
> 34:2].**

Observe carefully the words chosen to depict this judgment: *indignation, fury, utterly destroyed,* and *delivered to the slaughter.* They are
the strongest possible expressions that could be used. The judgment is
universal, and it is severe. It is not only the ". . . time of Jacob's trouble" (Jer. 30:7), but it is the time of the earth's travail. Our Lord spoke
of this as a time of suffering that will be unparalleled in the history of
the world. The seals, trumpets, and vials in the Book of Revelation all

intensify and confirm this. Whether you believe it or not, the earth is moving toward the judgment of God. Instead of a wonderful day coming for sinful man, a time of judgment is coming. As we look around us at our contemporary civilization, everything we see is going to come under the judgment of our Almighty God.

Their slain also shall be cast out, and their stink shall come up out of their carcases, and the mountains shall be melted with their blood [Isa. 34:3].

This description is to me the most terrible and repulsive in the Bible. I can't think of anything worse than this. It confirms what the Lord Jesus said when He was here and what the Book of Revelation teaches about a coming judgment upon this earth.

I realize that a great many people doubt this, which reminds me of an incident when a tropical hurricane broke on the Gulf coast several years ago. I traveled along that area several years later, drove for miles and saw entire sections of cities that the storm had taken out. Even after several years, nothing is there. I also saw places where jungle in the area was absolutely removed. I was told about an apartment house in the area where a group of people were living fast and loose. When they heard the warnings about the storm, they decided that they would not leave. They didn't believe the storm was going to be severe; so they had a big beer bust. Instead of evacuating, they all got drunk. They ridiculed the storm forecast, and they were all killed. You can do the same thing concerning the judgment that is coming on this earth. God says that judgment is coming, and it is coming.

And all the host of heaven shall be dissolved, and the heavens shall be rolled together as a scroll: and all their hosts shall fall down, as the leaf falleth off from the vine, and as a falling fig from the fig tree [Isa. 34:4].

When you see a little leaf fall from a tree, you can attempt to glue it back on the branch, but it won't stay and it won't live. Just as surely, judgment is coming, and you can't keep it from coming. There is only one thing you can do: make sure that you have a shelter. Listen to God and remember that the Lord Jesus is the shelter in the time of storm which is coming upon the earth.

IDUMEA, REPRESENTING ALL GOD'S ENEMIES

For my sword shall be bathed in heaven: behold, it shall come down upon Idumea, and upon the people of my curse, to judgment [Isa. 34:5].

God bathes that sword in heaven—that is important to see. When you and I take the sword down here, it is for vengeance or some ulterior motive. When God takes the sword, it is for justice and righteousness upon the earth. His sword is bathed in heaven, and it is going to fall in judgment.

Idumea is Edom, and Edom is Esau, and Esau represents the flesh. Esau represents all in Adam who are rebellious against God and His people. God said, ". . . Jacob have I loved, but Esau have I hated" (Rom. 9:13). God will judge Edom because they are against God, against His people, against His Word, against everything that is right and good.

INTENTION OF THE LORD

For it is the day of the LORD's vengeance, and the year of recompences for the controversy of Zion [Isa. 34:8].

This is the day of the Lord's vengeance. We will see this again in Isaiah 63:1–6. You can't do anything to stop it, just like there is nothing you can do to stop Niagara Falls from flowing. God says that things have to be made right upon this earth. To make them right He has to put down the evil and rebellious man upon this earth. Many people will not bow to God; but, since this is God's universe, where will they go? He has only one place for them, which is called hell. You may have your own concept of it, but it undoubtedly is lots worse than a place of literal fire. God's Word is inviolable and the Lord Jesus said, "Till heaven and earth pass, one jot or one tittle shall in no wise pass from the law, till all be fulfilled" (Matt. 5:18). My friend, it is wise to read the weather report and when a storm is forecast to make arrangements to escape it.

CHAPTER 35

THEME: The blessings of the Millennium, a picture of the kingdom

As we come to this chapter, we can thank God that the war of Armageddon is not the end of all things. Chapter 35 is a poetic gem. There is a high sense of poetic justice in this chapter which concludes the section on judgment. The fires of judgment have now burned out, and the sword of justice is sheathed. The evening of earth-trouble is ended, and the morning of millennial delights has come. This section closes on the high plane of peace, having been through suffering to peace, through the night to the dawn, through judgment to salvation, through tears to joy in the morning.

The calm of this chapter is in contrast to the storms of judgments of the previous chapter and even those that preceded it. We can say with the writer of the Song of Solomon, the winter is past, and the flowers appear on the earth.

MATERIAL EARTH WILL BE RESTORED

First we see that the material earth will be restored and the curse of sin lifted. This is the *body* of the earth.

> **The wilderness and the solitary place shall be glad for them; and the desert shall rejoice, and blossom as the rose [Isa. 35:1].**

We are informed today that the deserts of the world are being enlarged each year; they are not being reduced in size. Drought and soil erosion are hastening this process. Today pollution is filling the earth. All of this will be reversed for the Millennium. The smog will be lifted, and the curse of sin will be removed. The familiar and beautiful statement, "the desert shall . . . blossom as the rose" is an apt and happy picture of the earth's future. If you are familiar with the great desert area of the southwestern section of our country, you will be impressed with this statement. This outline was written while we were crossing the southeast section of Colorado where the drought has been so severe and where the vast grasslands have been eroded by sandstorms. During the Millennium all of this will be reversed.

> **It shall blossom abundantly, and rejoice even with joy and singing: the glory of Lebanon shall be given unto it, the excellency of Carmel and Sharon, they shall see the glory of the LORD, and the excellency of our God [Isa. 35:2].**

Paul tells us that creation is groaning and travailing in pain (see Rom. 8:22), while in the Millennium all creation will rejoice.

MEN WILL BE RENEWED

The bodies of men will be renewed, as will the psychological part of man.

> **Strengthen ye the weak hands, and confirm the feeble knees [Isa. 35:3].**

Creation is waiting for us to get our new bodies.

> **Say to them that are of a fearful heart, Be strong, fear not: behold, your God will come with vengeance, even God with a recompence; he will come and save you [Isa. 35:4].**

In the midst of the storm of judgment, God's people can rejoice because they will know that God will come and save them. The church has the added hope and joy of never experiencing the Great Tribulation Period.

> Then the eyes of the blind shall be opened, and the ears
> of the deaf shall be unstopped.
>
> Then shall the lame man leap as an hart, and the tongue
> of the dumb sing: for in the wilderness shall waters
> break out, and streams in the desert [Isa. 35:5–6].

Sickness and disease and all affliction are the result of man's sin.
These will be lifted in the kingdom.

> And the parched ground shall become a pool, and the
> thirsty land springs of water: in the habitation of drag-
> ons, where each lay, shall be grass with reeds and
> rushes.
>
> And an highway shall be there, and a way, and it shall
> be called The way of holiness; the unclean shall not pass
> over it; but it shall be for those: the wayfaring men,
> though fools, shall not err therein.
>
> No lion shall be there, nor any ravenous beast shall go
> up thereon, it shall not be found there; but the redeemed
> shall walk there [Isa. 35:7–9].

What a beautiful picture we have here of the earth during the kingdom
age.

MEMBERS OF GOD'S FAMILY WILL
RETURN TO ZION

Here we see the *spirit* of earth; that is, man will be renewed spiritually.

> And the ransomed of the LORD shall return, and come to
> Zion with songs and everlasting joy upon their heads:
> they shall obtain joy and gladness, and sorrow and
> sighing shall flee away [Isa. 35:10].

Can you think of anything nicer than this? This not only includes Israel, but it will include the redeemed who enter the Millennium upon the earth. In Zechariah 14:16–17 we read, "And it shall come to pass, that every one that is left of all the nations which came against Jerusalem shall even go up from year to year to worship the King, the LORD of hosts, and to keep the feast of tabernacles. And it shall be, that whoso will not come up of all the families of the earth unto Jerusalem to worship the King, the LORD of hosts, even upon them shall be no rain."

We can say with that old Puritan, Richard Baxter, "Hasten, O Saviour, the time of Thy return. Delay not, lest the living give up their hope. Delay not, lest earth shall grow like hell, and Thy Church shall be crumbled to dust. O hasten, that great resurrection day, when the graves that received but rottenness, and retain but dust, shall return Thee glorious stars and suns. Thy desolate Bride saith, Come. The whole creation saith, Come, even so come, Lord Jesus. The whole creation groaneth and travaileth in pain, waiting for the revealing of the sons of God."

Thus ends the first major division of the Book of Isaiah with all the blessing of the Millennium.

BIBLIOGRAPHY
(Recommended for Further Study)

Criswell, W. A. *Isaiah*. Grand Rapids, Michigan: Zondervan Publishing House, 1977.

Gaebelein, Arno C. *The Annotated Bible*. Neptune, New Jersey: Loizeaux Brothers, 1917.

Ironside, H. A. *Expository Notes on Isaiah*. Neptune, New Jersey: Loizeaux Brothers, 1952.

Jennings, F. C. *Studies in Isaiah*. Neptune, New Jersey: Loizeaux Brothers, n.d.

Jensen, Irving L. *Isaiah and Jeremiah*. Chicago, Illinois: Moody Press. (A self-study guide)

Kelly, William. *An Exposition of Isaiah*. Addision, Illinois: Bible Truth Publishers, 1896.

Martin, Alfred. *Isaiah: The Salvation of Jehovah*. Chicago, Illinois: Moody Press, 1956. (A fine, inexpensive survey)

Martin, Alfred and John A. *Isaiah*. Chicago, Illinois: Moody Press, 1983.

McGee, J. Vernon. *Initiation Into Isaiah*. 2 vols. Pasadena, California: Thru the Bible Books, 1957.

Unger, Merrill F. *Unger's Bible Handbook*. Chicago, Illinois: Moody Press, 1966.

Unger, Merrill F. *Unger's Commentary on the Old Testament*. Chicago, Illinois: Moody Press, 1982. (Highly recommended)

Vine, W. E. *Isaiah*. Grand Rapids, Michigan: Zondervan Publishing House, 1946.